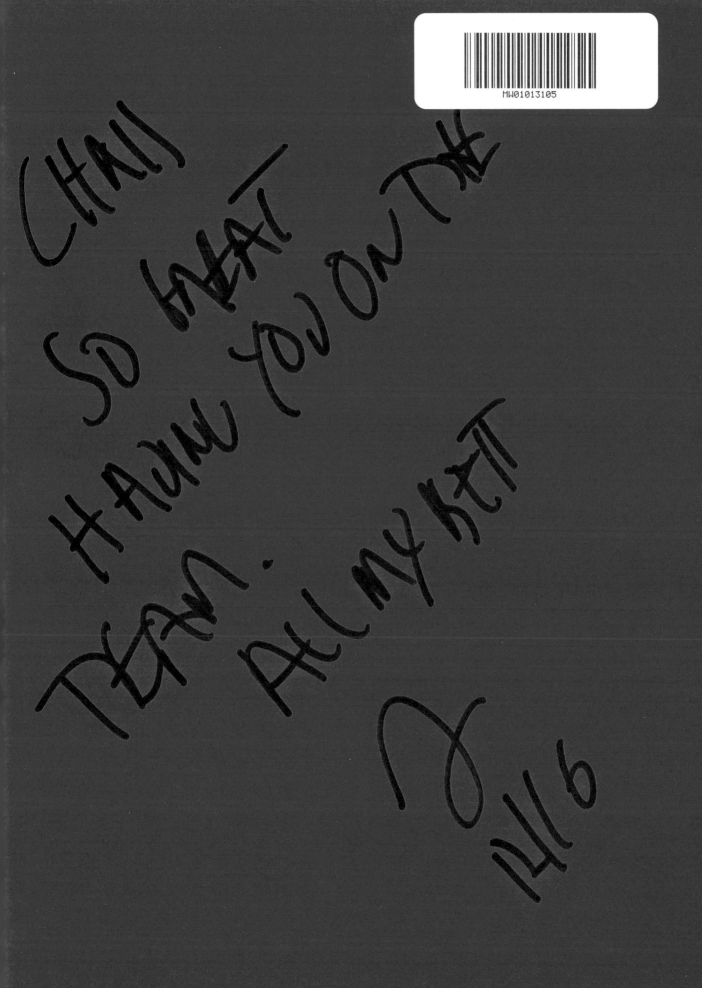

CHRIS
SO GREAT
HAVING YOU ON THE
TEAM. ALL MY BEST

14/6

RICHARD SAPPER

EDITED BY

JONATHAN

OLIVARES

For Richard and Dorit

RICHARD
SAPPER
EDITED BY
JONATHAN
OLIVARES

WITH PHOTOGRAPHY BY RAMAK FAZEL

"In truth, nature begins to relate to us only when we begin to indwell it, when culture begins in it. Culture then develops and, bit-by-bit, nature is refashioned. We create our own world, shaped by thoughts and controlled not merely by natural urges but by ends that we set to serve ourselves as intellectual and spiritual beings, an environment that is related to us and brought into being by us...Take a vessel sailing on Lake Como. Though it is of considerable weight, the masses of wood and linen, along with the force of the wind, combine so perfectly that it has become light...We have here an ancient legacy of form...We have here real culture—elevation from nature, yet decisive nearness to it."

ROMANO GUARDINI, *LETTERS FROM LAKE COMO*

PREFACE

In March 2008, while in the midst of compiling the book *A Taxonomy of Office Chairs*, I met with Richard Sapper to discuss the eponymous chair he designed for Knoll in 1978. This meeting took place in Richard's home office in the Brera district of Milan. Unbeknownst to either of us, this would be the first of many conversations he and I would have over the coming years, and it was the beginning of our collaboration on this book.

Our discussion revealed Richard's complex, considerate, and intuitive decision-making process. I learned that his Sapper Chair, made with rolled-steel profiles, was intended as a lifeline to a steel car-bumper factory he had nearly put out of business when he invented the plastic bumper for FIAT. When I inquired why so many of his products are black, I expected to hear some dogma about restrained visual expression, but I was pleasantly surprised when he stated that black is not only easy to clean but looks good in any environment, whatever the aesthetic climate. And when I asked why the leather upholstery of his chair for Knoll is folded into darts that close the leather in a decorative gesture, he became frustrated, as if I had missed something obvious. "Because it is nice!" he exclaimed.

Richard was preoccupied with the livelihood of his factory-owning friends. He was concerned about whether his objects would be kind to his customers' varied and personalized interiors, and he cherished both industrial processes and crafted details. His multifarious and human approach to design dealt with industry, craft, and interiors practically and generously. Within his working methods a manifesto had crystalized which I felt could be of great importance today. I asked Richard if we could collaborate on a book that would—through our trans-generational conversation—explore his life, work, and approach to design. He agreed.

Based on over fifty hours of conversations, the book is a definitive study of Richard's life and work, and comprises three parts: a photo essay of Richard in his living and working environments taken by Ramak Fazel; an oral history written by Richard and myself, which explores Richard's methods, motives, and the work produced over his entire career; and a visual chronology that features events in Richard's personal and professional life, products, exhibitions, photographs, writings, and significant publications on his work. The last two parts are cross-referenced with page numbers, allowing the reader to move between them. Collectively, these three parts explore Richard Sapper's life and work in the round, and like him, they don't draw too much distinction between professional and personal activity, or between work and play.

Ramak Fazel's photo-essay, "Domestic Contours," portrays the atmosphere of Richard's living and working environments in Milan, Lake Como, and Los Angeles. Halfway through my conversations with Richard, Ramak was hired by *Domus* magazine to photograph the Sapper residence in Milan for an article about Richard by Justin McGuirk. Richard worked from home offices throughout his entire career, and Ramak's candid photographs—all shot on a Rolleiflex TLR—capture the environment vividly. I commissioned Ramak to photograph Richard's other living and working areas in Los Angeles and Lake Como. Collectively, these images convey the environment from which Richard's products emerged, as well as the context of our conversations. As a nod to Richard's penchant for surprise—and to his victorious career, which took place south of his native Germany's border with Italy—Ramak has inserted a surprise of his own. This "fly in the ointment," as he calls it, is emblematic of the fact that this book is a project done between designers and a photographer, rather than a work of academic history.

The oral history is based on my conversations with Richard, archival interviews, and essays written by him. This section spans Richard's childhood; his interaction

with his early mentor, theologian and cultural critic Romano Guardini; his first job as a designer at Daimler-Benz; his subsequent move to Milan; his work in the office of Gio Ponti and at La Rinascente; his seventeen-year collaboration with Marco Zanuso; his major projects for clients such as Alessi, IBM, and Knoll; and his views on issues such as business and design, economy of scale, and design and society.

Notorious for his disinterest in speaking about his work, Richard preferred to let his products speak for themselves. While he might not be comfortable in a formal interview format, he loved a good conversation with friends, especially one fueled by some "fire water": Cynar or Punt e Mes, which he liked to serve on ice. Together in his Milan apartment, and at his family's Los Angeles home, we discussed his career chronologically, taking many long detours to speak about broader concerns and interests.

Richard's homes were an ideal context for our conversations. If he and I wanted to discuss a certain product, either he or his wife, Dorit, could always find it somewhere around the house. In Los Angeles, Aida chairs were located on the terrace, while La Cintura di Orione pots and pans turned up in the kitchen cabinets. In Milan, the Sapper Monitor Arm was clamped to his desk, and the Tizio lamp sat beside the living-room sofa. Many of his personal references—a prehistoric ax head, his grandchildren's drawings, and a note from the late graphic designer Alan Fletcher—decorated the surfaces and walls. Richard's homes and their contents were a fundamental part of our conversations and helped trigger his memories.

There were many projects that Richard felt were unimportant, or couldn't recall in detail, and so the conversation centered on the projects he was excited to speak about in the present. As is the case with any oral history, Richard's account is subjective, with all the biases, omissions, and possible exaggerations that come with a first-person recollection of events. For instance, he never had much to say about the "boxes"—Sapper-speak for televisions and radios—that he and Marco Zanuso designed for Brionvega, or the storage and office systems he created for B&B Italia and Unifor, respectively.

In tandem to our conversations I also studied all of his past interviews and essays, and found overlaps, additional information, and even information that contradicted our conversations. With Richard's approval, and permission from the original interviewers, I integrated the information found in the archival interviews and essays within his oral history. Wherever archival material is referenced, a footnote with the original source is provided.

The oral history is organized chronologically, divided by subject and interspersed with my own notes, which shed light on the context of our conversation, Richard's environment, and pertinent historical facts.

To create scaffolding for my conversations with Richard, my office assembled a chronology of his life and career, which was based on his own digital archive and the books, catalogs, and articles that have addressed his work. The chronology—assembled under the belief that design does not occur in a vacuum—shows Richard's work alongside key events in his personal life and career, personal photos, exhibitions, catalogs, books, essays written by Richard, and important articles on his work. It should be noted that the chronology is limited to images that were available to us; IBM and Lenovo's visual archives are scant, and many of Richard's products for these clients were never documented. While the chronology was developed as the basis of our conversations, here it is presented as a freestanding exhibit.

Reducing Richard's approach to a limited series of maxims would overlook the complexity and nuance that exists between his projects. However, looking back on our

RICHARD SAPPER

conversations, I feel that Richard's career does provide us with a manifesto of working methods that can be summarized as follows:

• He dealt with products of all scales, from pens to buses, and from objects made in low volumes to products manufactured in the millions. He sits comfortably in nonspecialist territory, and moves easily between differing projects of complex or simple natures.

• He dealt with manufacturers of all scales, from personal exchanges with family-owned businesses to corporate consulting within large organizations. As a professional, he was adept at maneuvering among the political land mines that lay within the development process of industrial design for hire. His business acumen, combined with his understanding of the function of beauty, gave him sway over industry in a way that few designers of his generation had, and as a result, he was able to assert his thinking over design of mass scale.

• His objects were often poetic, such as the 9091 Tea Kettle that rewards the user who cleans it by reflecting the world around it, or the ThinkPad laptop that hides a surprise (the keyboard and digital content) inside a simple black box. This approach, pioneered by Richard decades ago, moves beyond pure problem solving into matters of interest, which is where today's designer is most at home.

• Richard's products embrace a long tradition of man-made objects, and often reference features of pre-modern furniture, such as the armrests of his Sapper Chair, which echo the armrests of a wooden chair that has been in his family for generations. Richard's references were not postmodern visual puns; they are practical, and they engage a legacy of historical form in furniture while embracing functionality and modern technology.

• Many of his works involve movement, and visually express the gravity, rotation, and equilibrium that enable them. This approach takes advantage of natural principles, and offers the user a connection to and an understanding of them within the framework of the man-made object.

The aim of this book is to explore Richard's approach, the varying conditions, motives, and histories that surround and stimulate his process, and to extract from all of this a set of tools that are relevant for the practice of design today.

On December 31, 2015, in the final days of this book's production, Richard passed away in Milan. He leaves us with a rich body of work to draw from, and his personality, fondness of surprise, sense of humor, wit, and kindness survive in his products. I am grateful for his generosity, collaboration, and friendship.

PART I

DOMESTIC CONTOURS
BY RAMAK FAZEL

RICHARD SAPPER

RICHARD SAPPER

RICHARD SAPPER

RICHARD SAPPER

RICHARD SAPPER

RICHARD SAPPER

RICHARD SAPPER

RICHARD SAPPER

RICHARD SAPPER

PART II

AN ORAL HISTORY
BY JONATHAN OLIVARES
AND RICHARD SAPPER

Without traffic, it's only a twelve-minute drive from my office to Mathias Sapper's house in Los Angeles; Mathias is Richard's son. I take Route 101 North to the Gower St. exit, and then take North Beachwood Drive Blvd., which takes me into the Hollywood Hills. I will make this journey for the next three days for our first series of conversations. Mathias' driveway is the steepest I've ever parked in, and it is overgrown with jade bushes wrinkled by the dry summer heat and ongoing drought. Mathias—his resemblance to Richard is uncanny—quietly guides me down a pathway to a terrace, where Richard is waiting, dressed in his everyday uniform: button-up short-sleeve shirt, khakis, brown Top-Siders. Richard's wife, Dorit, is here, too. We enter the house and sit on a pair of black leather sofas, which surround a coffee table buried in magazines, drawing tools, papers, and an emptied FedEx box addressed to Richard from Lenovo, the company that has produced the ThinkPad since 2005. Evidently this is Richard's office for the week. Dorit and Richard purchased the house in 1990, while Mathias was studying at Pitzer College in Claremont, and it has been allowed to age; yellows that must have been vibrant are now pale, vegetation has done its thing, and the place is a charismatic mess. When I tell Richard that I want to discuss his ancestry and childhood, his eyes light up. Questions on design, I will learn, require some prodding to elicit lengthy answers, but on the subject of family, Richard speaks freely and passionately.

ADVENTUROUS
ANCESTORS

My father was born in Guatemala because my grandfather, Richard, had gone there when he was a young kid; it's an incredible story. My grandfather went to Guatemala because he and a friend had made a pact during their school years that if, once they had gone their separate ways, one of them should get lucky in life, he would invite the other to join him. Immediately after school my grandfather went into what was the family business of buying and selling spices. The spice trade brought him to Greece, which is where he was living when he received a postcard from his friend, and the postcard said, "I have found paradise. Come."

It turned out his friend was in Guatemala, and so my grandfather asked his father for his entire inheritance and used the money to board a steamship for Guatemala, which in those days took three months. But when he arrived, he discovered that his friend had died of yellow fever, and this left him with two choices: go back to Europe or continue inland, where yellow fever wasn't a risk. He ended up continuing onward to Cobán and there he began working for a coffee plantation owner. He eventually saved enough money to buy his own plantation, and in a very short time—maybe a year—he had bought so many coffee plantations that he was one of the richest men in the area.

And so my father, who was also named Richard, was the eldest of four children who were all born in Guatemala. He grew up in the jungle, with horses and mountains, but there was no school, so he was sent back to Stuttgart to live with his grandmother so that he could study. He was very sad to leave his paradise in the jungle behind, and the grandmother, she was very strict, so he was very, very unhappy.

My great-uncle, my grandmother's brother, who ended up looking after my father when he had moved back to Germany, had some very interesting adventures of his own. He had been working in the American West as a cowboy, but after some time he had had enough of the Wild West and decided he needed civilization, so he moved to New York City. He became an elevator operator in one of the first skyscrapers, the New York Life Insurance Building. While he was there, he befriended some of the big bosses of the insurance company, and one day they asked him if he would leave his elevator to somebody else and come into the office. He accepted and became an insurance agent. Soon enough, a year or two after that, he was one of the most successful insurance agents at the New York Life Insurance Company.

He made a hell of a lot of money, and at this point he thought he didn't need to work anymore. So he went back to Germany with his wife and spent his time playing golf. He also started to help his little nephew—my father— who was very unhappy in school. My father always told me that the only good times he had were when his uncle would visit. His uncle would come and do all things that you can do with a little boy: take him to the boxing matches and do big things with him.

Then came the First World War, and as my great-uncle had an American passport, he had to leave Germany or face prison. While crossing the Atlantic, the ship he and his wife were on was torpedoed by a U-boat! My great-uncle and his wife survived, but they had nothing left but their pajamas. So they came back to New York with nothing, absolutely nothing.

They had to start from scratch again and after the First World War, my great-uncle decided he would try his hand at selling automobiles, and that was a golden period for the automobile. He started to sell Daimler-Benz automobiles in New York, and as a result of that, he was rich again in a very short period of time! He retired in Stuttgart, but eventually ended up with multiple sclerosis. When I was a little boy, my great-uncle was semi-paralyzed, but he was my favorite. He was always, always positive, and always experimented. He always knew things, even if it was only how to feed the birds. He was just amazing.

CHILDHOOD

When I was a small boy my main preoccupation, my main problem, was that my father was gone because he had been drafted into the army. So in maybe the most critical period for a little boy to have his father, I had no father, because he was gone for eight years: on the front lines as a soldier. This was a terrible time for me because I was very, very attached to my father and I barely saw him during that time.

All the things that happened there, they naturally didn't leave so much space for my imagination, my fantasies of other things. I had more important things to think about. It was an horrendous time. The sounds of bombs and air-raid sirens kept us from sleeping almost every night. We had very little to eat. I remember very well the uniform of the Nazis, which was brown. It was really terrible, and then there was the SS, whose members wore black uniforms, and everybody was afraid of the SS. Then there was the army—the *real* army—who wore this field green. It was just awful.

When the war was finished nobody knew where my father was; it turned out he was a POW. All the mail and all other connections broke down and we had no infrastructure; you couldn't go from one place to another. There were no trains, there was nothing. Nothing was working, and it was also dangerous, and I was just a kid. And then my father came back, fortunately. *He came back.* My family, we were very lucky in the Second World War, because we were one of the rather few families in Germany that came out of the war intact.

It occurs to me that Richard was born in the same year as German artist Gerhard Richter and German designers Ingo Maurer and Dieter Rams, and that their generation bore the responsibility of reinventing their world in a new image after the blight of Nazi Germany. This was no small chore, but the sense of freedom—the blank slate—must have been exhilarating. It should also be noted that when Richard discovered design, the field was anything but mainstream. Dorit has told me that the word *design* wasn't even used when she and Richard first met in the sixties, and that Richard first came to know the profession as *Formgebung* (shaping). I ask him to explain why he first became a student of philosophy and business, how his diversion into design came about, and what the design profession looked like at that time.

My father was a painter, and I recall the day I was tall enough to see what was up on his working table, and what it was that kept him so busy. I was exposed to the arts at a young age, but if you asked my father what he learned at the academy, he always gave the same answer: how to sharpen a pencil. This may have persuaded me to seek out something more practical in my studies, and after I finished school in Stuttgart, I went to university to study philosophy. Why philosophy? Well, I was always attracted by it, but more importantly I didn't really know what I wanted to do, or what profession I should take. So I thought that maybe if I studied philosophy, I would get an idea of what to do. But I didn't graduate in philosophy; I graduated in business administration, because my father said I should have something in my pocket. I did my thesis in business administration. I never use that stuff any more, but it was there. Even though it didn't contribute to my creative development, these studies were important because they taught me methodological thinking and broadened my horizon.[1]

During this period while I was studying philosophy and business, I still didn't really know what I wanted to do. But I learned something about industrial design when a copy of Raymond Loewy's *Never Leave Well Enough Alone* ended up in my hands. At that time, I looked at the profession in the same way a lot of young people still look at it today: designer—what a great career. It has something to do with technology; it has something to do with art. You can create something yourself; there is no need to sit constantly at an office desk.[2]

It seemed to me that this would be a profession I would enjoy doing, but it was almost impossible to get information about the field because it was so new. It seemed to be a sort of risky endeavor, but it was very attractive. The forms of industrially made objects attracted me. You must remember that my father was a painter, and in my family it was normal to create objects with an aesthetic basis.

I decided to get to the bottom of this matter and tried to meet some people who were working as designers, but there were none I could find. I began to make more serious investigations and I found no more than ten people who worked as designers in Germany at that time. So I phoned them up and talked with some of them, and they all strongly advised me against entering this

[1] Piero Polati, "Intervista a Richard Sapper," in *Il Modello nel design: La Bottega di Giovanni Sacchi* (Milan, 1991).
[2] Richard Sapper, "Warum macht ein Designer Design?," in *Werkzeuge für das Leben* (Göttingen, 1993).

crazy career. Today I realize that their advice was well-founded, but at the time I didn't want to admit it. Then I read of the Hochschule für Gestaltung in Ulm. It didn't actually exist yet, but the foundation had just been laid. I drove to Ulm and talked to Max Bill, explaining that I wanted to study design, but he told me that I would have to wait a couple of years until the school was built. He told me all about his plans for the school, and said that he would invite me to the opening party once the new building had been completed.[3]

ROMANO
GUARDINI

At the University of Munich, Richard was a student of Catholic priest, theologian, and cultural critic Romano Guardini. *Letters from Lake Como*, written by the priest in the mid-1920s, offers a critique of the industrialization that was taking place in the region. "I have a plain sense that a world is developing in which human beings can no longer live," he writes, "a world that is in some way non-human." For Guardini, industrialized forms were incongruous with nature and eroded an ancient legacy of form that placed man in harmony with the natural world. He illustrated this point with a comparison of the sailboat and the steamship: the former represents an elegant mastery over the forces of nature that requires a proximity to, and deep understanding of, nature; the latter obliterates any trace of nature, allowing its passengers to go about their business without any engagement with natural forces. While it has been widely reported that Guardini helped steer Richard toward the field of industrial design, I want to understand the circumstances that led Richard to consult with Guardini, and why a theologian with negative views of industrialization would guide a young man into a practice that was increasingly rooted in industrial production.

If I had asked my father for advice on whether I should choose this or that profession, he would have said the decision was mine to make. This was not the guidance I needed, so I went to my philosophy professor, Romano Guardini, who was very old but very famous, and I asked him if I could speak to him about something. Guardini said, "Yes, come to my house tomorrow and we can talk."

At this time, the life ahead of me felt very uncertain. I could have gone one way or another. I had studied so many things in university—philosophy, drawing, anatomy, and business—and while I was excited by what I had seen of industrial design, it was far from an established career path. I needed the advice of someone I respected, whatever it was going to be. Either my ideas of being a designer were crazy, or Guardini could help me justify them to my family and myself.

So, I went to his house and started to explain what I wanted to do, and he was sitting there on the sofa and he started to speak. "Look at this beautiful thing I have here," he said. And that thing was a glass vase made by the Murano glassmaker Paolo Venini. Guardini said, "Look at this glass vase here: isn't it beautiful? Every time I look at it, it gives me joy." He went on to explain that if an object was capable of altering one's emotions, of transmitting joy in the

---

[3] Richard Sapper, "Warum macht ein Designer Design?," in *Werkzeuge für das Leben* (Göttingen, 1993).

world, then making objects of this kind must certainly be a noble act. But he also stated, "If that is the only thing you want to do in all your life, now that is another question."

He encouraged me to choose industrial design, but he was a theologist, so for him the most important thing was the spirit. He said, "If you want to do that as a profession, then you must know that for yourself." And I said, "Yes, I know that for myself," because I was very much attracted by design, and I thought that if I could get somebody like him to support my decision, then I would certainly carry through with it. And so I decided to become a designer and I'm still a designer. It was a very spiritual thing.

INDUSTRIAL DESIGN

In German universities, when you prepare for your exam, you speak about the thesis with your professor. The student has to select a thesis topic and the professor has to agree on the selection, and if they can't agree, there is no thesis. So I had to speak with my professor, and my professor was a great fan of industrial design. I gave my professor two choices. One was "The problems of coffee planting in Central America," which I was interested in because of my family's history, and the other was "The economical background of decisions concerning the selection of form" or something like that. And my professor said, "I'm not interested in coffee at all, but I'm very interested in design and in the economical problems of design," so the deal was done. I started to work on that thesis.

In order to write the thesis, I had to interview the companies that worked on design in Germany. There were not many, and one of them was Daimler-Benz, so I went to Stuttgart to interview the boss of automobile design, Karl Wilfert, about the problems of economic decisions surrounding form. He was a very nice guy and I interviewed him about this economic side of factory life and we spoke about this and that. At the end, we had developed a very good relationship by talking to each other.

At this time I was deciding what to do after my studies in business. Max Bill had actually invited me to the opening of Ulm, and I made the trip to the opening party. It was wonderful. In my whole life, I had never seen so many beautiful women gathered in one hall. I thought, this certainly is the right career for me! I was contemplating going to school there, but I had also kept in touch with Karl Wilfert at Daimler-Benz. I don't know if Wilfert ever looked at that thesis, but one day he asked me if I would like to work for Daimler-Benz—just like that. I said I would have to think about it, but why not? Yet there was one caveat: he said that I would need to study engineering for one year before I could start. Before I could work, I needed to know how to make technical drawings, but I was not interested in learning too much more than what I had to, in order to get this drawing job. So that's what we did.

DAIMLER-BENZ (1956–8)

Unlike that of so many of his German peers, Richard's education in design did not have roots in the Bauhaus or strong ties to Ulm. When I ask if Bauhaus or Ulm tactics factored into his early years as a designer, he shrugs and says, "My education was the automobile." In the late nineteenth and early twentieth centuries, German industrialists invented the automobile by adapting motorized coaches, and they developed a design approach of their own where aerodynamics, engineering, and the limitations of efficient steel-forming guided many formal decisions. At Daimler-Benz, Richard was immersed in this automotive culture, which had a powerful influence on his design career. Sectional drawing techniques, employed in automotive design, factored into many of his later works, and his romance with steel—a material with limitations that Richard would come to appreciate and master—began at Daimler-Benz. But Richard was also selective about which techniques from the automotive toolshed he employed. His use of motion was always appropriate to the object in question, and he never fell into the trap of giving everyday objects aerodynamic forms.

Afterward, I began working in the styling department at Daimler-Benz, which back then consisted of twenty people. The cars were designed within one single room and models were built life-sized. This room had only two doors; one led to the production hall where the prototypes were assembled, where access was restricted; and the other led to the outside world and had no door handle. Obviously the whole thing was confidential. The board of directors had to walk through that room, too, since there was no other way to see the models. As a result, they used to come through our workshop every day.[4]

There were always people, with or without their wives, who wanted to see what we were planning for the future. If we were to see an old Daimler-Benz from 1959 or 1960 on the street, I would be able to show you the following: Mrs. Chief Executive wanted to have this specific tail, whereas Mr. Director chose that precise chrome strip. After visiting our workshop, they would communicate their special requests. Depending on how charming the executive's wife was, our director made sure that these wishes would be more or less fulfilled.[5]

But that is how things were back then. For me, as a young apprentice, this experience was extremely interesting because I could witness the decision-making process in a major company firsthand. Some of these episodes I will never forget. I am going to tell you about one more. Once, a discussion took place between Professor Nalliger, who was the technical director for Daimler-Benz at that time, and his sales director. The sales director complained strongly about the squeaking brakes on all the Mercedes cars: "It is inappropriate to sell cars that cost twice the price of an Opel but squeak when you put on the brakes. You need to change the pads. This is scandalous!" To that, Mr. Nallinger replied: "You know, we use the best brake pads you can find. They just happen to squeak. We'll insert new ones only if we find pads that are just as good or better than these—otherwise not." This was a fantastic attitude: proof that this company only did whatever was considered truly right, and not something that conformed to a salesperson's desire.[6]

My first project at Daimler-Benz was to work on aspects of the 300SL Roadster [→ P.99]. The rearview mirror was just my first job, but I was working all the time; one week I might have been working on the rearview mirror and another week on the lower edge of the door. There were all these parts—many, many, many parts—and they all had to be designed and fit together. It was immensely complicated.

[4–6] Richard Sapper, "Warum macht ein Designer Design?," in *Werkzeuge für das Leben* (Göttingen, 1993).

RICHARD SAPPER

I learned many things in this environment, like how a car designer makes form, which is different from how other designers make form. They designed a form with many sections—every centimeter there was a section—and in all axes. When you have mapped out an object that way, you have a net, and this net shows you every point of the form. I used this technique afterward on a great number of projects, like the Lambda chair, for instance.

After a couple of years, however, the work ceased to be very exciting. I gave my boss a proposal about how Mercedes could change the way it designed cars, but shortly afterward he came back to me and said that my proposals were intriguing, but Mercedes would never make cars in the manner I proposed.[7] And so I had to do whatever it was that they wanted me to do. There was my boss, and then another five or ten bosses under him, and in the end there was nothing left for me to do but follow orders: "Draw that like that, draw this like this." It was that sort of relationship. It occurred to me that doing this for two years was OK, but that if I continued for twenty years it would be dismal. It was at this time I decided to move to Milan, where I had the feeling I would be able to test new waters.

It is the afternoon of our third day of conversations, which happens to be a Friday, and Richard and I are tired of talking. Another FedEx box arrives for him from Lenovo. The last one contained a 3D printing of a ThinkPad update that he had been advising on, and the new delivery holds an updated model. While I have been indulging in Richard's stories over the past days, my own office has gone unattended. As I pack up my notes, Richard expresses doubt about whether we will ever find the time to reach the proposed fifty hours of conversation; he suggests that perhaps I should instead speak with his clients to gain a better understanding of his work.

But a fifty-hour conversation with Richard is a project I feel I *have* to do—out of respect for Richard and his legacy; because of our growing friendship; because designers of different generations rarely take the time to do this kind of thing; because every year I meet design students who are unaware of his work; and for the incredible firsthand stories that might be lost if we don't sit down and talk our way through them. Fifty hours of conversation with Richard is not something I necessarily want to do, but it is something I feel an obligation to do; *we must do this project.* Richard understands this, and we find the time in our respective schedules for our next meeting, which will take place that coming autumn in Milan.

SEPTEMBER 2013, MILAN

MILAN (1958)

Dorit and Richard occupy the top two floors of a five-story, late-nineteenth-century building located between Castello Sforzesco and the Piccolo Teatro in the Brera district of Milan. A wooden gate leads me from the street to an open-air hallway and the porter's office. Once cleared for entry, I walk through a smaller enclosed hallway to the oldest elevator in the city: a tiny thing furnished in cast iron, carved wood, and red velvet. The elevator slowly climbs its way to the fifth-floor landing, where I find

---

[7] Steve Hamm, *The Race for Perfect* (New York, 2009), p. 70.

find the door to the apartment and a smiling Richard, who welcomes me inside.

Marco Zanuso renovated the apartment before the Sappers moved here in 1989, and it includes a studio where Richard has worked ever since. The interior is marked by nineteenth-century wooden furniture that has been in the Sapper family for generations, an abundance of books on shelves and in piles, Richard's father's oil paintings, his grandchildren's drawings, and some of his own designs. Like the Sappers' house in Los Angeles, the apartment in Milan possesses a special kind of cluttered warmth.

When Richard moved to Milan in 1958—at the age of twenty-seven and without speaking a word of Italian—German popularity had not yet recovered from its all-time low after the Second World War. Despite his disadvantages, Richard quickly found his way into the epicenter of the Italian design scene. Decades before the country's manufacturers worked with designers outside their borders, he produced a large body of work within the framework of Italian industry. I ask him to explain how he carved out this path for himself.

Milan was already very much known as a place where great designers were working. My girlfriend at the time was studying graphic design in Stuttgart, and she had an Italian friend who had lived in Milan and had come to study graphic design in Germany. This friend of hers offered to take me around the design offices in Milan, to introduce me to designers and interpret for me, because I did not speak one word of Italian. I said, "OK, wonderful!" So we made a trip together to Milan.

Milan felt very much like a city; it was a very busy place. Together we visited Gio Ponti and Ignazio Gardella. I hadn't really heard of these people before visiting Milan. The guy in Ponti's office who was in charge of industrial design was Alberto Rosselli. I had brought samples of the work I had done at Mercedes, and Rosselli looked at this and offered me a job. So I stayed in Milan.

GIO PONTI
(1958)

Whereas at Mercedes there were hundreds of German engineers of all types and all of them working together, the population of Ponti's office was maybe thirty young kids from all over the world, working in a single room, on a single floor of a big garage, all architects and designers. It was like a circus. Atmosphere is not to be underestimated. It couldn't have been more interesting, more positive; it was fabulous. I had found myself in a world that was soaked with cultural inspiration.

There were some wonderful personalities in the studio as well. I would interact periodically with Ponti, but really it was Rosselli who oversaw my work in the studio. I could not stop observing Rosselli: always extremely elegant, always a gentleman, with his big, dark, enigmatic brown eyes. There was also Gianfranco Frattini, who in those days drove to Ponti's studio in his red Alfa Romeo Spider, and wore ties with the biggest knots I have ever seen. I used to wonder, how can an architect make so much money?[8]

Rosselli would come to my desk asking, "What are you doing here? Can I see that?" By that time I still had almost no comprehension of the Italian

[8] Roberto Sambonet, *Richard Sapper: 40 Progetti di Design* (Milan, 1988).

language, so we communicated in English, which I had learned as a boy. The projects I worked on were chosen for me, but I had much more freedom to do as I saw fit than at Mercedes. We worked on a moped for a company in Naples, and I produced diagrams for it. Models and a final prototype were produced, but the company went bankrupt and the moped was never made [→ P.101].

After I had been in Ponti's office for half a year (or maybe three-quarters of a year), they didn't have much work anymore. They got into a crisis. Above all, they had a crisis of interesting work—at least for me, since I was not very interested in doing office furniture, and that's the only work they had to offer me at the time. I liked the studio; it was wonderful that a studio could be as nice as Ponti's was. But if the work isn't interesting, you move on.

LA RINASCENTE
(1958–61)

La Rinascente maintained its own in-house design team—Ufficio Sviluppo (Development Office)—from 1955 to 1964. During that time, Alberto Morello, who operated as the office's headhunter, came to hire some thirty designers from Finland, Germany, Italy, Japan, the Netherlands, and the United States, including several young talents who would become well-known names in the profession; Mario Bellini, Italo Lupi, Enzo Mari, and Richard.[9]

I started to look around for more work, and one of the places I found was La Rinascente. They had something that was called the Ufficio Sviluppo, and this was the brainchild of the owners of La Rinascente. It was another circle of young people from all over the world, who were working in Milan, and they were working on the objects that La Rinascente would offer. So I took a job there.

The projects we worked on were generally fast. There was a large team in place, but we would work individually, and I had a lot of freedom in that environment. La Rinascente didn't have an internal model maker, but we worked with an external model maker whenever we had the need. One of the first projects I worked on was the hair dryer [→ P.103], which was produced in bright-red plastic. This was a very fast project, but we managed to do something interesting: for instance the on/off switch was located on the handle so that the user could use it with a single hand, and the handle blended into the fan box in a way that gave negative space for the fingers. I worked there over the next three years, and perhaps worked on some fifty products. None of the projects I did were signed by me; it was not the idea to do projects with a name.

COLLABORATION
WITH MARCO
ZANUSO (1959–77)

I worked at La Rinascente for half of my time, and during the other half of my time I agreed to work with Marco Zanuso, which was a small office, with only about three or four people. Zanuso was an absolutely extraordinary personality, a wonderful man. I would drive between La Rinascente and Zanuso in a Lancia that I had at that time. Cini Boeri was working in Zanuso's studio at that time, and she and I became friends as well.

[9] Alberto Morello, "Looking for Evidence," in *Werkzuege für das Leben* (Göttingen, 1993), pp. 35–6.

Once Zanuso and I traveled to the US together, to California, for a new airplane seat we were developing with Boeing for Alitalia. But it was a completely ridiculous idea, because the upper spheres of Alitalia have always been corrupt, and they didn't care about anything we were doing. They asked us to design this and that, and we made models and prototypes, but they would never produce anything. If the management of an airline says they want a new airline seat and you give them a new airline seat, you expect that something would come of it, but nothing ever did. They ended up choosing an airline seat from the company that would give them the biggest financial kickback. But it was my first trip to the US, and it was fantastic, even if the work we did was never realized.

There wasn't some eye-opening thing about working with Zanuso; you can't look at it that way. It was the overall culture, which was so stimulating and gradually left its mark on me. We ended up collaborating for seventeen years.

Zanuso and I thought very differently, but our dialog was always stimulating and resulted in interesting things. While his thinking had a strong artistic dimension, my own background was technical and I was primarily concerned with practicality. While he looked at the form, I always tended to reflect on the structure of a thing and how it should function, or whether it moved and, if so, how it should move. The combination of our methods gave our clients what they needed. Perhaps the Lambda chair and the radio for Brionvega [→ P.109] are most emblematic of our collaboration. He was a mentor, collaborator, and great friend and I learned many things from him.[10] We remained close until his death. The last project I did with Zanuso was his project for my apartment in Milan.

The 1960s would be the most prolific period in Richard's seventeen-year collaboration with Marco Zanuso. Together the pair would co-author numerous groundbreaking products, including the stamped metal Lambda chair for Gavina, the TS 502 radio for Brionvega, and the K 1340 children's chair for Kartell, which was the first chair made from a single piece of injection-molded plastic. During this period Richard would also receive his first independent commissions, which kicked off his own design practice. The first of these commissions was from the owner of Lorenz, a company that had been founded in 1934 in Milan, as a manufacturer of timepieces.

STATIC (1960)
[→ P.105]

In his first independent project—the Static table clock for Lorenz—Richard's interests in metal manufacturing and harnessing movement play out. The form was milled from a solid block of stainless steel with a counterweight to keep the clock perched upright, and causing it to roll back into its upright position should it be knocked over. The Static won the Compasso d'Oro in 1960, when Richard was twenty-eight years old. The award—the most prestigious prize given to products in Italy—was founded in 1954 by La Rinascente, and was based on an idea of Sapper's earliest Milanese colleagues, Gio Ponti and Alberto Rosselli. Richard, still a new transplant to the country, was already solidifying his place in Italian design culture.

[10] Michael Webb, *Richard Sapper: Compact Design Portfolio* (San Francisco, 2002), p. 13.

It was not my idea to do projects under my own name. You have to realize that then, and even now, some companies would rather not announce their designers because they're afraid this might cost them money. But some companies began to realize that if they wanted to have good products, they had to work with designers. This is how I received my first independent commission, which is an interesting story.

At La Rinascente they had a secretary who I guess was a bit in love with me. And one day she received a call from an entrepreneur who had a company that made clocks. He confided in her that none of his products had ever won the Compasso d'Oro and he wanted to know how La Rinascente had gone about doing so. And so she told him, "Well, you don't have good designers. You have to hire a good designer to win the Compasso d'Oro." And he said, "Yes, but how shall I do that?" She said, "Well, maybe I can propose somebody." And she had me in mind.

She appeared at my desk and said, "There is a man who would like to speak to you." And I said, "Oh? Why?" And she said, "He wants you to design a clock. Would you be interested in that?" She explained the circumstances of why he had called, so I said, "Maybe." And she said, "OK, I will call him and then you can talk to him." I told her that I couldn't promise to win the Compasso d'Oro but I could try. And finally, a short time afterward, maybe the next day, she came and said, "Here is Mr. Bolletta [Tullio Bolletta, founder of Lorenz]."

Richard takes a long pause in our conversation, his eyes focused on his hand as he gently rubs his knee. Whether he is recalling details or daydreaming I have no idea, but I take the time to look around the apartment. I take in photographic books on Japan's Katsura Imperial Villa, Picasso sculptures, and China; the biographies *Nicholas and Alexandra* and *Peter the Great* by Robert K. Massie; stacks of dated *National Geographic*; CDs of Beethoven's Ninth, Mozart's *Requiem*, Schumann's Piano Concerto, and Bob Dylan's eponymous debut album; and hand-carved and painted wooden animals (a leopard, a tiger, a horse). A few minutes go by, and then out of nowhere Richard jumps back into the conversation, picking up exactly where he left off.

Mr. Bolletta had a problem, which he explained to me. During the war, they had produced torpedoes with internal clock mechanisms that would run the torpedo for the time necessary to get the torpedo to where it should go. After the war, naturally no one wanted the torpedoes anymore. And so Mr. Bolletta had bought, at a very good price, a railway car full of these torpedo clock mechanisms and now he wanted to make clocks for people out of those. I said, "Well, let's have a look." So I looked at [the mechanism], and I studied the problem, and the problem was not so easy because these mechanisms were pretty big and needed a battery, which increased the size even further.

I thought about it, and I designed a clock that fit these big sizes. I proposed to Mr. Bolletta to make this clock, the Static, and he said yes, wonderful. It was quite difficult to make, because you could open the clock only from the front; the rest was a single round piece of turned metal. Then it has this flat spot, which is cut into the volume, for the clock to rest on the table. When you tip the clock over, it would roll on the table, until it found the flat part, and then it would stand upright again. So that was "the game" of that clock.

For the clock's face I needed a typeface, so I went to the flea market looking for typefaces, and I found a clock face from a bomber plane. It fit my clock perfectly! So my clock's face was based on this one.

It was exciting when the Static won the Compasso d'Oro, but I wouldn't say that it made my life less or more difficult. I just kept going. I kept my personal work separate from my work at Zanuso's office, working on my own projects from my apartment. I was also entering a very busy period with Zanuso.

LAMBDA
CHAIR (1963)
[→ PP.110–11]
& GIOVANNI
SACCHI

We made the Lambda chair for Gavina. It was a truly original object, conceived by applying the technology of automobile body construction to the design of a chair. I was familiar with this process from my time at Daimler-Benz, which consists of stamping and spot-welding steel sheet parts, which are then spray-painted like an automobile body. We also had another version made in stainless steel with a leather cover. Only 500 or so were ever made before the production was discontinued.

If I remember correctly, this was the first project I developed with the great model maker Giovanni Sacchi.[11] It is important to get a three-dimensional version of the project as quickly as possible, in order to give it a body, a volume. You need a model maker you are very much synchronized with. I have known each of the model makers I have worked with as if they were my brothers.[12]

I continue to work almost exclusively in a three-dimensional process. I would often start with a cardboard or plaster model, and this would express the concept I wanted to develop. I would make this model only for myself at first, and then study it before completing the design in the form of a sketch. Then I would take this sketch to the model maker, who would make a more precise wooden model. At this stage, if the model was good, we would make another model, repeating this process until we would be sure that we couldn't make a better one. And the one model that can't be improved any further, and that convinced me thoroughly, would be used to present the idea to the client.[13]

This is a task that any good model designer could carry out, but the collaboration with Sacchi was one of decisive importance for many reasons. I could go to Sacchi's workshop and say, "Let's make a model in such and such a way," and they knew exactly what I intended to do and what I wanted to do. I didn't even have to provide drawings or explanations. And everything would always work out fine and they would save me an enormous amount of time.[14]

During all these years, Sacchi spent Sundays and nights working on models I couldn't have found anywhere else. This required an absolute commitment to work that characterized not only him but also his collaborators. I could go to his workshop and say that I needed to take a model along to the United States in three days; three days later I would get my model. The essential point is that there is an atmosphere of perfect balance and friendship in the workshop, and this (I am repeating myself) is the most important thing to me.[15] I always need models, and I need first-class model makers. I cannot do anything with

[11] Piero Polati, "Intervista a Richard Sapper," in *Il Modello nel design: La Bottega di Giovanni Sacchi* (Milan, 1991).
[12] Lance Knobel, "Richard Sapper: Breaking the Silence," in *Designer's Journal*, November 1985.
[13-15] Piero Polati, "Intervista a Richard Sapper," in *Il Modello nel design: La Bottega di Giovanni Sacchi* (Milan, 1991).

somebody who is not first-class, because these models are shown to people who have to decide whether or not they will make an investment. If they decide badly or negatively because the model is made badly, that is a very bad situation. The way technology is going with 3D printing, in a relatively short time, you may not need model makers anymore. But who knows? The story rarely develops the way you think; we might see a completely different outcome.

K 1340 (1964)
[→ PP.114–15]

For me, personally, the "decade of plastics" began in 1963. In that year Giulio Castelli, owner of Kartell, asked Marco Zanuso and me to design a chair made in a single piece of injection-molded plastic, using a material that was extremely market-friendly, polyethylene. The result of this request was a little chair for children, the K 1340, the first injection-molded plastic chair in the world, which won the Compasso d'Oro in 1964. It was a revolution, even if it would take many years for industrialists to be convinced, that a great number of the objects we find in our daily lives, which were traditionally made in wood, ceramics, or other materials, could also be made in plastic.

Why were they ultimately convinced? Because plastic costs less. And this reason hasn't changed. As of yet, nothing has happened to stop the phenomenon of the injection-molded plastic that constitutes a great part of our built environment, starting with toys. How has this invasion changed our lives? Above everything else it has changed colors. While wood and metal have their own inherent colors and require painting to change, which costs money and labor, plastic can be made in any color without spending anything extra. As a result, our world has become much more colorful, a phenomenon that has had captivating and positive effects, which anyone can witness walking into a toy shop.

As our conversation continues and evening draws near, Richard seems a little restless. Then an excited look comes over his face, "I have an idea!" he says, and he disappears into the adjacent room that leads to the kitchen. A few minutes later, he comes back with a stainless-steel tray carrying bottles of Punt e Mes and sparkling mineral water, bowls of ice, olives and pine nuts, and a cup loaded with grissini and exclaims, "Let's have some fire water!" Richard explains that while Punt e Mes is almost unknown today, it was a very popular drink when he was young. "Cynar is another thing. If you haven't tried it, you should." He mixes our drinks and starts in on the pine nuts. This elegant little ritual gives Richard a great deal of pleasure, and his love of spontaneity and of being a good host shows through vibrantly.

MOBILE
HOUSING
UNIT (1972)
[→ P.129]

The mobile housing unit was produced as one of a series of commissioned environments for the MoMA exhibition *Italy: The New Domestic Landscape*, which was curated by Emilio Ambasz. Participants in the exhibition, which included Gae Aulenti, Mario Bellini, Enzo Mari, Alberto Rosselli, and Ettore Sottsass, among others, were asked to respond to a brief written by Ambasz titled "The Design Program," which is a highly complex paper that came with a few attachments and a long list of recommended reading. The gist of the brief is that designers were to work on private, private-communal, or communal environments that were fixed, fixed-adaptable, or adaptable, and they were to execute these environments in partnership with Italian industry, exploiting the potentials of synthetic materials and fibers. The exhibition split designers into two camps: those who aimed to mold behavior patterns with practical solutions to issues of urbanity, poverty, or disaster; and those who, "despairing of effecting social change through design," deferred to staging events and issuing polemic statements. Richard and Marco Zanuso's contribution falls in the former category, and is the only work on an architectural scale the pair created together.

Emilio Ambasz, curator of *Italy: The New Domestic Landscape* [→ P.128], asked Zanuso and me to contribute to the exhibit, and we were really allowed to do what we wanted within the philosophical background of the exhibition. It was so enjoyable to get to do what we wanted! It was a wide-open period, open to the future. This was one of the more important projects that Zanuso and I did together. It was a lot of fun to do. We worked on it for about half a year.

We created mobile housing units based on 20 ft. (6 m) freight containers. These were meant to provide housing for communities displaced by large-scale construction or a catastrophe, like a typhoon or earthquake, or for tourist environments where nature must be preserved and therefore construction is prohibited. The freight container module allowed effective transportation while protecting the interiors. And the units could be unpacked and opened up for use in just a few minutes. Each unit had an electrical system, water tank, and waste-disposal tank, and the idea was that the units would be powered by generators, receive water from an external supply, and that refuse would be removed by trucks.

You had the basic container, then you could pull out a piece here or there, and you had your kitchen, or your balcony. We dropped the side walls so we could have a terrace on both sides, and windows and doors. It was a little house! We furnished the interiors so that the whole unit would be pre-made. We inserted pre-molded fiberglass elements for the bathroom, the kitchen, a closet, and the sleeping area. FIAT, Boffi, and Kartell were invited to take part and they accepted and helped realize the project. They helped to make all the fittings, but otherwise it was a regular freight container. You can do this with any freight container, but the model for the exhibit was only taken so far. There were materials, like particleboard, used for the prototype, which would have never held up to the elements.

I went to New York for the opening of the show and it was quite an opening! Many friends had very interesting proposals in the exhibit, too. Alberto Roselli did an interesting mobile home for recreational purposes. Sottsass, for instance, had all those refrigerators! It was a time when technology promised to do so many things. Some thought that technology would solve all of our problems, particularly the Americans; others thought technology would only deepen our problems. I sat somewhere in the middle of that debate.

We had studied the logistics, so that a 10,000-ton (9,072-tonne) ship could provide housing for an entire community, or move a community from one coastal location to another. And the individual units could then be moved into place by helicopter. They could use these today in the Philippines![16] Today

[16] Richard was referring to the 7.2-magnitude earthquake that struck the Bohol province of the Philippines on October 15, 2013, when thousands of structures were damaged and more than 200 people were killed.

we are living in more difficult times than then. There are situations where the designer has to help society move toward change.

I believe that FIAT held on to the models that were made for the show for some time. We didn't know if we would influence the future with our design; we just did it. We were curious. We thought something would come out of it, but nothing did! Very often it's like that. You can have a stupid or boring project—nothing new—but you just do it, and then it is a big success. And then you can work with the most serious and ambitious intentions, and nothing really comes out of it.

PIRELLI & FIAT
(1970s)
[→ PP.134–5]

A little-known fact about Richard: he invented the plastic car bumper that revolutionized the way cars were—and still are—made. Prior to his research for FIAT in the seventies, car bumpers were manufactured with steel, a heavy and rigid material that damaged vehicles as much as it protected them. Richard's shock-absorbing plastic bumper was molded as part of the car's form, instead of being added as a separate element, as steel bumpers were, and it offered superior protection for cars in light collisions. Within a few years of his groundbreaking work, the plastic bumper had become ubiquitous and the steel bumper was downgraded to a specialty item, only used for heavy-duty vehicles. The car bumper is the first of many instances, including his later work for Knoll and IBM, where Richard inserted himself into the mechanism of large-scale industry and effected wide-reaching change.

At about the same time as *The New Domestic Landscape*, I was working as a consultant to Pirelli on advanced pneumatic structures. This was a special program where we explored a pneumatic belt made from a rubber tube that would be placed all around a car body. The idea was that you could be driving at low speeds, and the pneumatic belt would absorb the shock of a collision against a light pole or object. We were able to prevent damage at this speed successfully, and even prevent injury to a person who might be struck at this speed. We had developed this idea in conjunction with FIAT, but they realized that the cost these structures would add to the vehicle far outweighed the financial benefits of having them. Yet they hoped to get some legislation passed that would require automobiles to implement these safety structures. And they almost succeeded in having a law passed that would require vehicles traveling at nine miles (15 km) per hour to be able to hit a wall or pole without showing any damage. But at the last minute, just as we were gearing up for production, the law was canceled, and as a result the pneumatic belts were also canceled.

After the law was canceled, we said, "OK, let's do something simpler." We designed a plastic bumper that absorbed much more shock than the steel bumpers that were the standard in those days, and took on less damage under light collisions. Actually, Renault had introduced a fiberglass bumper with the first model of its R5, but these were rigid, and we were the first to use an elastic plastic. The cost advantages of our approach were substantial. Within a few years, a great portion of the auto industry had turned to plastic bumpers.

By the early seventies, Richard's work with Zanuso was winding down, and he began taking on more independent commissions. The Tizio desk lamp was the first product he created independently that achieved widespread international success, both critically and commercially. It employs several methods that would become signatures of his approach, such as an expressive kinetic structure and the use of new manufacturing technologies to redefine an existing archetype. The thoughtful employment of the color black enables the object to blend into varied environments and to mask seams between components. The Tizio draws on more than twenty years of mastery in designing in steel that Richard had attained and would continue to develop. Richard also used the color red to highlight an important control, a signature that he would use on several future projects, such as the ThinkPad, Sapper Chair and Sapper Monitor Arms. I ask Richard to explain the genesis of the idea behind the lamp, and the development process that brought it from concept to final product.

I had met Ernesto Gismondi at a cocktail party in the sixties, but my introduction to Artemide, his company, came in the early seventies, when he approached me and asked if I had ideas for new products. Gismondi and I are about the same age; when we met he was an entrepreneur with a great deal of enthusiasm and engineering knowledge. Over the years we became great friends; we have had some exciting moments sailing together. Anyway, I had designed a table clock (Tantalo) [→ P.126] some years before he first approached me, which had never been produced, so I gave the design to Artemide and they released it.

Gismondi had also asked me to design a work lamp. I thought about what I would want in such an object, and designed one based on my own personal needs. While working, I like it when the light falls directly onto the table, directly onto the sheet of paper where I am drawing, or the book I am reading. And I prefer to have the rest of the room dimly lit. On a normal lamp, one has to place the shade or the reflector near the head of the person sitting at the table, and that is not very comfortable as it is unwieldy and large.[17] So the lamp had to cover as much area as possible, but without taking up a large footprint. There wasn't a lamp that embodied all these characteristics, so Gismondi's challenge was appealing.[18] I thought then that I would try to design a lamp with the smallest possible reflector that wouldn't bother me when it was near my head.[19]

Another problem was that I am a very messy person. There is no space on my desk to put a lamp, or the only location would be at the farthest corner of my desk because the rest of the surface is heaped with things I probably don't need but that I can really only deposit on the table. For that to work, you would need a very long swivel arm. Being able to move a lamp easily is a mechanical problem, you would need to find a structural system, a mechanism—whatever you want to call it—that allows you to move a small but distant reflector without any resistance. You can use one of two existing systems: a swivel arm with a spring or one with a counterweight. It was clear to me that a counterweighted arm would be the more natural way to reach my goal than a spring-balanced

[17] Richard Sapper, "The Process of Design," in *Pacific Design Center News* (Los Angeles, 1987).
[18] Hans Höger, *Design Classics: The Tizio-Light by Richard Sapper* (Frankfurt am Main, 1997), p. 11.
[19] Richard Sapper, "The Process of Design," in *Pacific Design Center News* (Los Angeles, 1987).

one. But it was not simple to implement this plan mechanically. When you want to deploy long swivel arms within a balanced system and you start with a reflector of a certain weight, and you keep in mind the series of steps necessary to retain the required degree of freedom, you end up with enormous weights. And so the underlying design problem of the Tizio was to save weight. That complicated the design of the reflector because it had to be extraordinarily light. And it required very fragile position and swivel arms because they had to be spindly and thin in order to save weight. This then resulted in a mechanical problem with the connecting hinges, because if such a lamp fell or was bumped, the arms could permanently bend. It was necessary to make a connecting hinge that would release in such an emergency.[20]

I needed a durable connecting hinge that could conduct electricity and produce a minimum amount of friction. And I needed a joint that was very cheap and easily movable. After I looked around for a bit, and after designing a bunch of very complicated movable connecting parts, I discovered that a press stud was most suitable, such as one used to fasten a jacket or parka. It turned out that this was the right means to my end.[21] I believe that was it, mainly because setting the transformer into the foot was very simple, and so I built the prototype of the lamp.[22] I worked completely by myself, made the prototype, and when it was ready I brought it to Gismondi and put it down on his desk. When I switched it on he immediately saw the potential of the thing, so Artemide produced it very quickly.

The lamp is black, and I still make many things in black because it is a color that always looks good when put into contrast with other colors and environments. It looks good in a modern interior or an antiquated interior. You have to study the use of black looking at automobiles. Look at the same automobile in gray, in black, in white, and you will find that in black, the disturbing details, seams, and cracks are far less visible.

What drives me in all of my design work is the desire to find a logical solution to a problem I have noticed. A problem I have either encountered in my own life or that could occur in other people's lives. I then try to find a logical solution to this problem. And that is really, I think, a very matter-of-fact, prosaic interest. But there are absolutely no indicators—before or after the work is done—to tell you whether the undertaking will be successful or not.[23] In my opinion, it is necessary during the development process to have a kind of filter that separates the sensible solutions from the equally sensible ones that give formal expression to the thought illustrating the solution and the problem behind it.[24]

HEUER (1976)   The products that Richard designed for Heuer were an important precursor to his later designs for IBM, and there are many parallels to be found between the two bodies of work. For Heuer, Richard oversaw a series of visually related electronic products, and with the Microsplit 520 stopwatch [→ P.138] he first conceived of the hinged box that would become the underlying concept of the ThinkPad.

[20]-[4] Richard Sapper, "The Process of Design," in *Pacific Design Center News* (Los Angeles, 1987).

I designed a stopwatch for the company Heuer [now TAG Heuer] in Switzerland. Back then, an atmosphere of change prevailed in the field of electrical engineering, and this company was one of the first to understand that the era of the mechanical watch was coming to an end, and that industrial design was absolutely necessary to survive in the marketplace.[25]

The design of the watch only took me four months. Usually I require at least one year between the date of the assignment and the finishing of a product. After six months, the profiles were ready and, one month later, they could use it. All in all, eleven months: a record time. When the watch appeared on the market, it contained an electronic system that was three generations ahead of other watches; it worked better, only cost half as much, and required only a tenth of the space that I had originally planned for the watch's shape. At the beginning of my professional activities, the production of an integrated circuit required more or less nine months and a capital expense of several million dollars. By the time I was working with Heuer, it could be done in three days. One ended up wondering how to work under these circumstances. Nowadays, a designer's work is very difficult; unless you design coffee machines or chairs, their designs don't tend to change quickly.[26]

The collaboration with Heuer was a very good project for me, because the toolmaking was Swiss. It was extraordinary that the pieces are just plastic, but perfectly made. And the Microsplit 520 was very important for me. The arrangement of parts, with the batteries in the front and the push buttons and controls under the lid—this all seemed logical at the time, but this arrangement became a sort of a guide for all my laptops. I mean, this is a small box, but dimensions aside, it's like a laptop; it contains electronics. You can open and close it. You can carry it around. The screen on the Microsplit 520 was so dim that you could barely read it. I also made the first digital stopwatch for Heuer.

At this point Richard and I have been meeting for evening sessions at his apartment in Milan for the better part of a week. The sessions have been intense and focused, and Richard, now eighty-one years old, speaks with the determination of a man in the autumn of his career who wants to set the record straight and he probes his mind for important details.

Jacques Heuer was a great guy and an extraordinary person, and we spent a lot of time together. He was a great person to work with, because of all that he knows, and all that he stands for. Well, my best clients become my friends. Now and then, there's one that I cannot hook onto, but there are not many. It's not that friendship is a prerequisite for good design work, but it helps. I have had projects that were a fight from the first moment to the last, where the client was really just uninterested. In a circumstance like this, it takes more work to develop the idea, so it costs more, and that type of client doesn't like that.

[25–6] Interview with Michele de Lucchi in *Ufficio Stile* 14, No. 4, 1982.

ALESSI & 9090
(1978)
[→ PP.142–3]

We haven't spoken about Alessi yet. It is one of Richard's longest-running and most fruitful collaborations, and is an enormous topic for our conversation. But this is my last evening in Milan, so we only have time to begin discussing this chapter in his career. We start with how the relationship began and his first product for the company, the 9090 espresso maker.

My projects for Alessi are planted into the sky; they are completely new objects that don't exist before I begin work on them. So I can never predict how long it will take, and there is usually no deadline. We just try to make a new product as fast as is possible. When I work on big projects for big industry that have a schedule, or have to be finished by next month or by next Saturday, then I have to work in a certain way. But very often I work on projects that do not have a real schedule; we are just aiming for the right results, and this can take years. Often, I have to develop a new technology to do that thing that I want to do, and this takes time, and sometimes we work for years until we have everything defined.

Alberto Alessi first came to me on the recommendation of my friend Ettore Sottsass. I don't know exactly how it came about, but from what I understood, Alberto had asked Ettore about me, and Sottsass had told him that the things I made were never wrongly done. He was a character, but his recommendation certainly went a long way. You know the designers here in Milan, at least at that time: we all knew each other. We would see each other when there was an opening for an exhibition that we were all interested in, or if there was a design award to be given out. So Alberto came to me and he asked me if I would like to design something for him and he offered me to design...I think it was tableware. And I said OK, and I did. The factory that was supposed to make the tableware was so bad that I told Alessi that he had better look for somebody else for the tableware project. So the project was canceled and I told him I would prefer to work on something else, and I offered him the coffee machine, which became the 9090.

The 9090 is the first design I did for Alessi, and it was really through this project that we got to know each other. I'm not a big coffee drinker; I would say I'm a normal coffee drinker. Alessi didn't make a coffee machine at that time, and Bialetti's Moka Express, which was being produced in the millions each year, dominated the market. We had to compete with that, which wasn't easy. In order to succeed, we had to produce the 9090 in large numbers and at very low costs. You could find the Moka Express in almost every Italian home at that time, but it had some flaws, and a dangerous aspect, because the top was screwed onto the bottom; if the safety valve malfunctioned, the pressure would build and the machine would turn into a bomb. This was rare, but every so often you would hear about an explosion in somebody's house![27]

The most revolutionary aspect of my design is the way it is locked. If you want to open the thing, you simply lift the handle, and if the pressure gets too high, the handle's latch comes undone and releases the pressure safely. It was

[27] Francesca Appiani, *Design Interviews, Richard Sapper* (Mantova, 2007), p. 31.

also important for me that the user was able to open it with one hand, without touching the hot coffee maker with the other. There was also a problem of planned obsolescence with the Moka Express; if you forgot it on the heat, the plastic handle was likely to burn and the whole thing had to be replaced. The metal handle I used solves this problem. So there were a few areas where there was room for improvement over the traditional model.[28]

I made the first models of the 9090 out of paper and cardboard, and then I worked with Giovanni Sacchi to make more advanced models; he made all of my models. I remember we made twenty or thirty different models in order to study the proportions. But after these initial models, which I used to present my ideas, Alessi made most of the prototypes.

The 9090 is manufactured with over ninety molding operations, but these steps are fast and economical, and the number of operations gives the object complexity. The 9090 has a form that expresses something about itself. It's a little steam engine, which is much more amusing than a coffee pot that disguises the fact that it is a quite complicated machine.[29] The intention is not to tell some story that can be relayed through words. But I believe that an object must somehow be capable of talking with someone who might look at it, and translate its sense to a user or an owner. The product was commercially successful almost immediately after its release. We made three sizes and one electric version, the RS07 [→ P.207].

The 9090—like the Tizio lamp, the Sapper Chair and the ThinkPad—has had enormous commercial success; to date, more than two million units have been sold.

During our conversations this week we have been sitting in Richard and Dorit's living room on a sofa and armchair; these are made of black leather and fastened together with metal studs. I realize that I have never seen these designs before, so I ask Richard about them. He explains that they are models he and Marco Zanuso designed for Arflex a long time ago, though he can't recall when exactly. The design was never produced, but Richard kept all the prototypes, and they have aged nicely.

Tomorrow I return to Los Angeles, and we agree to see each other the next time I am in Milan, at some point later in the year. As a parting gift Richard gives me a couple of rare books published on his work; *Werkzeuge für das Leben* [→ P.190], edited by Uta Brandes, and *40 Progetti di Design* [→ P.178] by Dorit Sapper, Donata Cocchi, and Roberto Sambonet. This is perfect reading material for my fifteen-hour journey home.

NOVEMBER 2013, MILAN

SAPPER CHAIR
(1978)
[→ PP.148–9]

The Sapper Chair has been in continuous production for more than thirty years, and as I learned in 2008 when I first met Richard to discuss it for my book, *A Taxonomy of Office Chairs*, the design relied heavily on his automotive manufacturing knowledge. We haven't seen each other since the autumn, and Richard is always a little reluctant at first to speak about his old work, as he prefers to talk about whatever he is working

[28] Francesca Appiani, *Design Interviews, Richard Sapper* (Mantova, 2007), p. 31.
[29] Lance Knobel, "Richard Sapper: Breaking the Silence," in *Designer's Journal*, November 1985.

on at the moment. His reluctance to go over the Sapper Chair is compounded by the fact that he remembers speaking with me about it six years earlier. But in our many sessions I have discovered a method for breaking the ice, a way into any conversation with Richard: he loves talking about people. And so I ask him who at Knoll commissioned the Sapper Chair.

Bobby Cadwallader, who was the president of Knoll International at that time, called me and asked me to design a new office chair; I believe it was 1975 or so. He was a very lively guy, very enthusiastic. He was from Texas, I believe, and with a big Southern accent, and was always in Italy for one reason or another. We had a great time working together on that chair, which I believe got started in 1975 or so. I would say that he became a good friend, although we haven't spoken in years.

But before I can tell you about the office chair, I must first remind you about the work I was doing for FIAT at that time, where I had been involved in the design of a new bumper program that resulted in the first plastic bumper. In a very short period of time—as a result of my invention—the steel-bumper industry was in trouble, as almost overnight the auto makers were adopting the cheaper plastic variation, which was more resistant to bumps and so on. When you have some ideas in your head from one type of work, it's natural that they cross over into other activities. Through my work for FIAT I knew the owner of a steel-bumper factory in Turin. And then, when I heard that they were having financial difficulties, I gave them the structure of this chair to do.

The chair was partly developed in the States and partly developed in Italy. It took about three years to complete. I made prototypes, and I would bring these to the US. In Italy, where we did the leatherwork, you find people who are excellent craftsmen and I had an upholsterer—a very good one. The upholstery was very traditional, but I developed a unique closure for the leather so that it would attach to the steel frame. This way you could develop the frame and the leather separately, and then in a third operation put them together. The people at Knoll developed the technical aspects of the closure.

The tooling for the Knoll Sapper Chair was very expensive. But you know, with steel, when you have the right production numbers and the right machinery, the unit cost can be *very* cheap. This is also what allowed the chair to be produced in big quantities. Knoll used an Italian producer to make the frame and with three workers they could make 2,000 chairs a day.

At the time that I designed the Sapper Chair, I held the belief that more and more of us were spending most of our lives in the office, but that the office was not improving at all. The application of ergonomic standards, at least in the way that manufacturers were applying them, tended to transform the office into something that looked like a hospital. You had ergonomists demanding legal regulations, to the point that the computer industry was producing height-adjustable terminals, and the furniture industry was producing height-adjustable workspaces, and the redundancy was absurd.

I felt that the office could look more like the living room. One of the most difficult things about designing for offices is that there is no average user. In the seventies and eighties, about the only thing you could be sure of was that he or she would sit on a chair and use a desk, and today you can't even be sure of that! Outdoors, if you have a good landscape, you don't need good design because there is enough beauty provided by nature. But in the office, you need good design, because if the objects around you can provide some pleasure, then you might feel a bit better at the end of the day.[30]

PUBLIC TRANSIT
STUDY (1972–9)
[→ PP.132, 146–7]

In advance of this meeting, I have told Richard that I want to discuss all of his works that have dealt with public transit. I have had an old text of his on this subject, originally written in German for the book *Werkzeuge für das Leben*, translated into English. Richard hasn't seen this text in a while, and periodically throughout our conversation he picks it up and reads directly from it. His work in this area includes a study for urban transit done with Gae Aulenti, a design for a moving walkway, a bicycle umbrella, a bus for bicycles, and a folding scooter that would eventually lead to his Zoombike in 2000. When I ask what problems he thought we faced in urban transit today, he wryly answers: "You will have to write a new book."

My interest and concern with issues of urban transportation began in 1972, when the Milan City Council commissioned Gae Aulenti and me to do a study on this subject. It was evident that the automobile was an almost indispensable part of our central European life, but that, over time, it had advanced to become the enemy of the big city.

At the turn of the last century the automobile liberated cities from the filth of many thousands of coach horses. But by the 1970s, it had become apparent that the car could only co-exist as a means of mass transport within the structure of a large city, such as in Dallas or Los Angeles. These cities subordinate themselves to the spatial requirements of car traffic, and thus forsake one of the essential character features of the city: the formation of a social center and the associated structures—homes, offices, shops, theaters, restaurants—which in turn generate encounters and stimuli. In other words, the big city can only live in peace with the car when it negates itself. It was evident that this was only possible, although hardly desirable, in developing countries, but had to be ruled out in Europe for historical and urban reasons.

The project we did began with an analysis of the required daily commute time and was explained in a series of topographic maps, where the same distance covered through different means of transport was represented in a scale of one minute equals two centimeters. Thereby, the actual speed of various transport systems could be compared directly. The example showed a typical commute from an apartment in the close outskirts of Milan to the office in the center of town, mapping the average transport time actually required, and, as an experiment, recorded graphically. We mapped and compared various commuting routines; driving, parking, and walking; walking, taking a bus, taking the metro, and then walking; biking, taking the metro, and then walking; and biking. Then we mapped these exact same scenarios, imagining that they

[30] Lance Knobel, "Richard Sapper: Breaking the Silence," in *Designer's Journal*, November 1985.

were augmented with a high-speed moving walkway, buses equipped to transport bicycles, and a hypothetical collapsible kick-scooter.

I kept developing these ideas further after the initial report. In total the work comprised a wide range of proposals and projects, including bike tracks and moving walkways; a folding steel bicycle with small wheels for [Dutch bicycle manufacturer] Batavus; a bicycle umbrella to protect riders from bad weather; a folding scooter; and finally the lightweight aluminum folding bicycle, Zoombike. I presented all of these ideas at an exhibition at the 1979 Milan Triennale, except for the Zoombike, which came later.

The Institute Battelle in Geneva, in collaboration with Dunlop, had developed a moving walkway for airports that could have been used in cities and placed under covers to protect pedestrians from rain. It had a speed of about nine miles per hour (15 kph), which, taking into account the additional movement of the user, increased transportation speed to an effective 12 miles per hour (20 kph): that meant a speed with a value comparable to a bus or tram. Since the walkway is always moving, waiting times could be eliminated completely, and therefore over short distances much shorter journey times could be achieved than with traditional public transportation. But there were obstacles: opposition toward the creation of visible infrastructures that could lead to an aesthetic deterioration of historic centers; and high levels of investment.

The "bicibus" was a bus equipped to carry commuter's bicycles that I proposed as part of my work in the Department of Research and Development at FIAT in 1974. The main part of the vehicle was to be designed like an aircraft fuselage. It had to be self-supporting, which would have eliminated a chassis under the vehicle floor. The wheels needed to be the smallest-possible diameter; the disc brakes were positioned next to the wheels, as in airplanes or racing cars; the suspensions, at least at the back, were to be independent from each other. The drive would be powered by electric motors, which were connected directly to the rear wheels in order to save space for a differential gear; the batteries were to be charged by a diesel generator or by power supply as in trolleybuses. The storage space for bicycles was to be allocated in the front, below the elevated driver's cab, so that the driver would keep direct control over the loading and unloading of bicycles. The compartment for bicycles was small and the bus held a lot fewer passengers than a traditional bus. The bus therefore had to run more often, which in turn would have resulted in shorter journey times since waiting times would be reduced.

The belief was that the additional cost for such a bus would be easily offset by the fact that no investment in infrastructure was necessary, and it did not require any decisions that would have had any irreversible impact on urban planning. But my conclusion was that the development and purchase of these new buses would have been very expensive and would have required difficult political decisions. So I tried to achieve the same result in an even simpler way: with a collapsible scooter.

For the 1979 Milan Triennale, I designed a collapsible scooter, which was modeled by Giovanni Sacchi and engineered by Cane Profilati. My objective was to design an individual means of transportation that could allow a speed of 12 miles per hour (20 kph), and at the same time fold in less than five seconds into such a small format that it could be taken onto every form of public transportation. This new vehicle had to be simple to use, so that as many people could use it as possible; however, the dimensions and the geometric design also had to ensure optimal safety when driving and braking. These characteristics required the greatest-possible flexibility of use. The model scooter that was exhibited was also the conceptual basis for the Zoombike, a commercial folding bicycle that I would realize some twenty years later.

IBM (1979)

In 1979, more than two years after its consultant design director Eliot Noyes had passed away, IBM was still searching for a designer to fill the role. Between 1956 and 1977, Noyes had been engaged in an extremely broad scope of activity, from designing specific products and setting an overall industrial design language, to overseeing graphics, architecture, and curating the company's art collection. The search for a new design consultant was more focused. As Paul Rand had taken over direction of graphic design, and IBM's facility building and art-collecting days were largely behind them, the company needed someone who specialized in industrial design. The new design consultant would need to provide conceptual and visual direction for new products, oversee a complex system of interrelated products (mainframe and midframe computers, typewriters, printers and emerging categories such as personal computers) and lead the company's fourteen design teams that were located in the US, Europe, and Japan. After assuming this role at IBM, Richard would design new computing archetypes almost entirely by himself, become something of a design coach to IBM's designers, and begin an international design collaboration that would last more than thirty years.[31]

In 1979, I received a call from my friend Paul Rand, who was the graphic designer and packaging consultant for IBM. He told me that IBM was searching for a new chief industrial design consultant, and that they hadn't had one since Eliot Noyes died some years before. I had met Noyes once or twice—possibly at the Aspen Design Conference—but not in any extended capacity. I had also met Charles Eames many times in California, who had also worked for IBM.[32] My answer to Rand was, of course, yes, and after a few meetings in Milan and New York with Rand and some executives from IBM, we signed the agreement [→ P.151].

Before joining IBM, I worked for Brionvega for twenty years designing television sets, which are more or less the same, and as ugly, as computers. I remember back in the 1970s, I said that when they introduced the flat screen, I would design the next television set, thus giving up that awful box I didn't want to deal with anymore. So you can imagine how I felt when they asked me to design computers.[33]

The first thing I did was to take a survey of what was being done at IBM in terms of design, and what I discovered was a very difficult situation: it was a complete mess! There were redundancies everywhere you looked; none of

[31] Author's conversation with Tom Hardy, December 29, 2015.
[32] Richard had met the graphic designer Deborah Sussman, who later worked in the Eames office, in 1958 when she was working in Milan. He also met Charles Eames in Los Angeles on more than one occasion, and had visited Charles and Ray at their home with his wife Dorit. He considered Charles to be a friend and something of a "father figure." Speaking about Charles, Richard stated, "It wasn't just that he was an extraordinarily good designer, it was his whole outlook on life that made him so exceptional."
[33] Interview with Maurizio Giordano, 1997.

the design managers were actually designing anything; and there was a gap between the managers' thinking and the junior designers' work. It was a mess aesthetically, but it was also a mess of duplication. There existed a corporate design manual that was meant to unify the various design efforts within IBM, but every location I visited had its own way of operating. Of course, at the time these things were possible because IBM made so much money from its mainframe computers that it could permit itself any stupidity in the world, and it would come out all right. But for a design consultant, this was not an easy situation.[34]

When Richard started working with IBM, the company had fourteen design centers: Austin, Texas; Böblingen, Germany; Boca Raton, Florida; Boulder, Colorado; Endicott, New York; Fujisawa, Japan; Hursley, UK; Kingston, New York; La Gaude, France; Poughkeepsie, New York; Raleigh, North Carolina; Rochester, Minnesota; San Jose, California; and Tucson, Arizona. Later, centers were also added in Charlotte, North Carolina and Lexington, Kentucky, and the Fujisawa center was eventually moved to Yamoto, Japan. Each location was positioned next to the facility that manufactured its designs—so, for instance, network terminal displays were designed and made in Raleigh, North Carolina, and disk drives were done in San Jose, California.[35]

The first project I worked on was the IBM Upright Typewriter [→ P.154]. IBM wanted to do a basic update of the classic Selectric typewriter, but I proposed something else altogether. It was to be an upright unit that cleared desk space and placed the paper much closer to the user, making it easier to read. There were new electronic displays coming from Japan that I wanted to use on the front of the typewriter. But this whole effort only taught me more about the problems at IBM; the executive review board discontinued the project under the justification that design quality only impacts sales by two percent, and why should they spend their money changing their existing typewriter. Of course, this was the last typewriter they made. The first IBM PC came out shorty afterward and the typewriter was dead.[36]

   To give you a sense of how disorganized IBM was at that time, I had no idea that the IBM PC was even being developed! It was a horrible design, a stupid, boring box. I disliked everything about it.

Because of the sprawling nature of IBM, during Richard's first couple of years at the company there were design efforts going on that he was unaware of. One of these was the IBM PC, which was developed by an IBM skunk-works engineering team that operated outside of the industrial design program. Because of the mounting pressure

[34] Steve Hamm, *The Race for Perfect* (New York, 2009), p. 71.
[35] Author's conversation with Tom Hardy, December 29, 2015.
[36] Steve Hamm, *The Race for Perfect* (New York, 2009), p. 71.

for IBM to release a personal computer to compete against models like the Apple II, the IBM PC was fast-tracked into production on a twelve-month schedule. As a result, most of the ideas developed by the industrial designer assigned to the project were swept aside in favor of a cheaper, engineer-conceived assembly of mismatched parts.[37]

The 5140 [→ P.168–9] was the first design I made for IBM that was produced. When it is closed it is a simple box, and then the screen opens up and reveals the keyboard. In profile the device looks like an alligator [→ P.170]. This was an internal joke between the designers in Boca Raton and me, because the area was infested with alligators!

IBM has a very changeable history with design. They had times when they were very careful of their prestige and they were employing good architects and doing good work, and then there were times when they absolutely couldn't care less. IBM has always been a very problematic thing, because while there were great people who were wonderful to work with, for every one of those there were four other bean counters whose only concern was keeping costs low and increasing profit. I always tried to avoid having to deal with the bean counters. Whenever I was in a situation like this, I tried to find out who, out of the people I had to deal with, was the most open to my ideas and the least difficult to integrate. Then they could become my ally. That was always my technique.

I paid no heed to the style of this large company; instead I tried to design it myself—with success. At a certain point when we were developing additional portable computers, I had come to the conclusion that all of IBM's portables should be black, not only because of the benefits I described earlier with the Tizio, but because this would help IBM stand out from the competition, who all used this awful beige color. But I was having great difficulty convincing the product bosses in Florida that we should adopt black. Eventually I became so frustrated that I took the issue to IBM Chairman John Akers. I asked him to look at the two computers side by side, and we forced him to choose, and he chose mine. I think from that point on I was the most hated man in Boca Raton![38] Eventually my philosophy won over and all IBM computers were changed from that hideous beige to black.

The work I was doing for IBM was like nothing I had ever done before. All of a sudden I had to do a hell of a lot of talking, whereas before I didn't have to do much talking.[39] I was also sending and receiving sketches with a fax machine, and at one point, before we began using email, we would send color photographs of models back and forth on a Sony device. Sometimes I designed things from scratch all by myself, other times I collaborated with designers within IBM. Often I was critiquing work that had already been done, which I would do in product reviews every few months. Over time I turned around IBM's entire product philosophy. It took me a good ten years, however, until I was actually able to push anything through. And then that was only because at

[37] Author's conversation with Tom Hardy, December 29, 2015.
[38] Steve Hamm, *The Race for Perfect* (New York, 2009), p. 71.
[39] Lance Knobel, "Richard Sapper: Breaking the Silence," in *Designer's Journal*, November 1985.

some point IBM was no longer able to explain why they were selling the Think-Pad so successfully. So they commissioned a market analysis, which revealed that a third of the people that had bought the ThinkPad had done so because of its design. This was something that had never occurred to IBM. Eventually they began to take what I was doing seriously. But I wasn't particularly happy about this because the real reason behind IBM's change of attitude was the increase in sales. And this was never my intention. I've never gone along with Thomas Watson Jr.'s thesis that "Good design is good business," for if this were true, then there would be no ugly products, but in fact there's any number of them; and they even sell well.[40]

Together with Tom Hardy, IBM's design manager who was Richard's principal contact within the company, Richard would participate in quarterly design reviews with IBM's designers. At each review, one or two designers from each of IBM's teams would convene at a single design center, and over the course of a few days Richard, Tom, and the designers would critique all of the work that was being done and then establish next steps. Richard and Tom gradually reshaped the product design protocols at IBM, making it easier and faster for the company to bring innovative products to market. Between the individual products he designed, and his regular coaching, Richard's influence at IBM and Lenovo have had wide-reaching effect.[41]

Beyond the most successful products that Richard spearheaded for IBM, such as the Mod. 5140 convertible personal computer, the ThinkPad, and the Netvista X401 desktop computer [→ P.203], one of the projects that had the most lasting impact on design at IBM, and subsequently Lenovo, were the "personality studies" [→ P.185] that he did in 1991 and 1992. These volumetric models, made independently of any specific product, established guidelines for dealing with overall geometries, fan vents, and touch points, while leaving room for interpretation among IBM's design teams. These studies influenced hundreds of IBM and Lenovo products, and their essential features can still be seen on models produced today.

SPAGHETTI
FORK (1981)
[→ P.155]

The Spaghetti Fork came out of a week-long conference organized by Alessi in Berlin. Alessi had invited a group of designers who had all worked for the company, and asked us to create something for ourselves to use while eating. You could do whatever you wanted, and so while we were there, in an atelier, I built this model myself. I was interested in the connection between manners around eating and the shape of a piece of cutlery. Italians swivel their spaghetti around a fork, which takes a foreigner many an Italian holiday to master. I wanted to make this easier for Germans by introducing a mechanical element that wound the spaghetti up in a single gesture. Then there was the fact that my friend Ettore Sottsass was there in the workshop, and he was wrapped up in the Memphis Group at that time, and so I took the opportunity to poke fun at him by

[40] Stephan Ott, "You Have to Rely on your Instinct!" interview with Richard Sapper, Goethe-Institut, June 2009, http://www.goethe.de/KUE/des/prj/des/dsn/stu/en4739094.htm.
[41] Author's conversation with Tom Hardy, December 29, 2015.

placing a roman temple at the top of the fork. It was a fun week, though I never intended the Spaghetti Fork as a product; it was more of a joke.[42]

ECONOMY
OF SCALE

Richard's work is synonymous with industrial production. While the seventies were a period when friends of his (namely Enzo Mari and Ettore Sottsass) took detours from industrial design to explore experimental or craft-based means of making work, Richard stuck to industrial production as his medium. Eventually, with IBM in the eighties and nineties, Richard engaged in design at a scale of production beyond what any of his peers in Italy achieved. I ask him to describe his position on design during the years when many of his contemporaries turned toward counter-design, radical design, or the Memphis movement, and to explain why he stayed committed to industrial design at a time when it was not particularly fashionable among his peers.

I never felt any connection with movements like Memphis. Even if my best friends were involved—Sottsass was naturally and always a great artist and whatever he touched, he touched well—I found that some of the products made by this group were horrible. I couldn't do anything about it, but for me, this kind of work was hiding from the fact that big corporations are where the movement is. Our economic situation depends on big things—not tiny things you show off for three days and then they're gone. So I have always been interested in relationships with companies where I could make *millions* of pieces, because I think design can only work when it's in big numbers. If it's not in big numbers, it won't work. When I say "work" I mean that, for a design to function, it has to have an effect on our lives. And this only happens if it is bought in big numbers. This is a basic fact of industrial design. It's the economy of scale.

Working with corporations, I have had to have many dealings with executives. If an executive chooses to touch design, he has to make aesthetic decisions, and there are many executives who are not interested in this or are afraid of it. An executive risks his life every time he puts on a tie! The blandest tie comes with the least amount of risk. Another executive issue is always cost. In the modern economical climate of the US, for instance, if any detail costs half or a quarter of a cent more, you have to justify it. In such a situation you can never make great work.

The newest technologies are sensitive to big numbers; the Internet is a grand example of that. Through the Internet, you can reach many, many more people. This is conducive to big numbers, but I am not so sure that is so good. If everything is big numbers, life gets boring. In general, I can say that I have never been interested in imposing limits on my work. Today when I design something, I have the problem of the environment on my mind, and I am trying to be as positive as possible in that regard.

There are projects where designers work with their hands. I think it is very natural that you try to make things with your own hands. The fact that most

[42] Richard Sapper, "Warum macht ein Designer Design?," in *Werkzeuge für das Leben* (Göttingen, 1993), p. 113.

of my products are made by machines...well, this just came about. It wasn't that I set out to work exclusively with these processes. The designer has to choose what interests him, and I have certain areas of products that interest me more than others.

However, this is somehow limiting the quality of the work, because if you do everything in the best-possible way, it really doesn't make a difference what you do. It's not that designing a motorbike is different from designing a sofa. I would say, given the choice, I am more interested in designing a motorbike than I am in designing a sofa. But if I had to design a sofa, I think I could be capable of designing a good sofa just by applying what I know, and my instincts.

People have asked me many times if there is a product that I have never worked on that I would like to work on, and this question I always answer with, "I would like to design agricultural machines," because they have such a strong personality. But a designer doesn't always get to choose these things. The most important thing for me is to give everything I do a form that expresses something. It's not neutral; it has a point of view and a personality.[43]

APRIL 2014, MILAN

9091 (1983)
[→ PP.160–1]

Today, Richard and I meet in his home office, at his desk, which is entirely buried. Obscuring the desk top area are a cup filled with Japanese pencils, an electric pencil sharpener, sketches, bits of plastic that look as if they could correspond to some product, a tape dispenser, a scientific calculator, a stack of books and newspapers, Richard's Tonga salt and pepper mill [→ P.220]. The sounds of rustling papers and chairs moving on the wooden floor fill the first moments of our meeting, then we get down to the order of business: first, the process behind the Alessi 9091 kettle and Richard's largest product family for Alessi: La Cintura di Orione.

The 9091 came along because after we did the coffee machine, everybody was asking for a water kettle. The agent of Alessi in Germany came to me and he said, "We need a kettle. We don't have a kettle." Without him they probably wouldn't have done anything, but this guy was really pushing for the kettle, and so Alessi started to work and to move, and so we made it. In Italy, kettles didn't exist! But every household in northern Europe used them to boil water.[44] I thought this might be the occasion to make something fun. Why can't a teapot give people pleasure and fun?[45]

The 9091 is a completely separate product from the 9090. I've never thought much about the relationship between the two objects, and I do not have a routine process that would connect them. But the process of design is

[43] Steve Hamm, "Richard Sapper: Fifty Years at the Drawing Board," in *Bloomberg Business*, January 9, 2008, http://www.bloomberg.com/bw/stories/2008-01-09/richard-sapper-fifty-years-at-the-drawing-board
[44] Francesca Appiani, *Design Interviews, Richard Sapper* (Mantova, 2007), p. 36.
[45] Lance Knobel, "Richard Sapper: Breaking the Silence," in *Designer's Journal*, November 1985.

quite complex, because you have to find a form, and the form has to work and it has to work from all points of view, so it's pretty complicated. I would say that I almost always start this process with a drawing.

The idea with the 9091 was to give it a special value when it is clean. It is shiny. It is clear. It looks spectacular when it has been cleaned, and I wanted to give people who have that kettle a sort of a reward for treating it well. Then there was the whistle, which was a project in itself. I'm always interested in connections to natural phenomena, which you could say leads us to the whistle. I didn't like the whistles of the average water kettle; they were shrill. But to achieve a lower sound you need more space than a water kettle has available. I went into a long period of research, looking for the right instrument that could produce a good sound, but it was very difficult, because everything I tried had to be very small.

Then it occurred to me that a pitch pipe could be just the right thing, as they give low sounds. These are tools used for tuning flutes, so I thought, why not use it as a steam whistle? I started to search for a supplier, and my sister, who at that time was a journalist in Germany, said that she might know somebody who made them. Eventually she found this guy in Bavaria, and she asked him if he could sell us some of his pitch pipes, and he said, "Yes, yes, I could. How many do you want?" So we asked Alessi and they said, "Well, for the beginning, 10,000." And the supplier said, "10,000? Now I can't go on a holiday!" His pitch pipes are still used for the kettle today. You have to listen to it; there are two pitch pipes, each in a different note, mi and si [ti], so it produces a harmony.

LA CINTURA
DI ORIONE (1986)
[→ P.174]

La Cintura di Orione is a big body of work that I did for Alessi over the course of several years, which is a full range of professional-grade gourmet cooking pots and pans. During the design process, Alberto Alessi, Alberto Gozzi, and I went on a long expedition through France, going from one famous restaurant to the next. We visited many of the most famous cooks in France. It took two weeks to make this trip and we asked them for advice on specific questions; they gave us their advice. And we ate much too much!

The French chefs that Richard, Alberto Alessi, and Alberto Gozzi visited were: Alain Chapel, Gualtiero Marchesi, Raymond Thuilier and Jean-André Charial, Angelo Paracucchi, Pierre and Michel Troisgros, and Roger Vergé. These chefs all appear in the 1987 publication *La Cucina Alessi*, happily using the products that were ultimately designed by Richard. I ask him to describe the manufacturing process for these pieces, and, because many of the objects in this collection serve highly specialized functions within professional kitchens, I also ask how he felt about designing products that he might never actually use himself.

The basis of the collection was a new technology we developed, which was a layering of metals; a thick layer of copper on the outside, and a very thin layer of stainless steel on the inside. You see, copper has an ideal and evenly distributed conductivity for cooking, but because copper is poisonous you can't let it come into contact with food. So we found a way to fuse the copper with

RICHARD SAPPER

the thin layer of stainless steel on the inside of the pot. We laminated these two materials, one on top of the other, and then put the whole thing through a stamping process. You get a pot that is stainless steel on the inside and copper on the outside, and this thing works very well. It took us—Alessi's technicians and I—a long time to get that thing going so that it worked well enough to be able to produce that stuff.

The material, the color of copper, is extremely beautiful, especially the way it ages, which is spectacular. Where the stainless steel of the 9091 was meant to be polished and reflective, I knew the copper Cintura di Orione would age beautifully, and gather a patina. There are also people who try to clean it, but that's not the right thing to do. The handles are made of heat-treated oxidized stainless steel, which was a material process I was familiar with from the development of the 9090. I didn't like how the handles on traditional pots ended abruptly—too crudely—so I introduced a circular handle end with a scoop.

In reality, I actually cook very little. My capabilities in cooking are mainly making steaks or cooking fish. But I'm interested in my objects, whether I use them or not, and I'm especially interested in them if they are something I would use, but most of the time I work on products that I may never, in fact, use myself. For instance, one of the pots I designed, maybe the most extreme pot in the whole collection, is for cooking enormous fish, which even the most advanced cooks don't do very often.

TEACHING
(1985–96)
[→ PP. 167, 181, 199]

Regular teaching is not something that most successful designers make time for. Dorit has explained to me that Richard was never interested in teaching until his friend Paul Rand convinced him to do a summer course with Yale graphic design students in Brissago, Switzerland. She has also said that Richard's students at the State Academy of Art and Design in Stuttgart adored him. I want to know something about his approach to teaching, and so, looking over some old descriptions of his course syllabi, he explains his techniques.

As in all creative professions, that of the designer must fight with a special difficulty: one can't really learn it. Specifically, one can, of course, learn knowledge, skills, and attitudes that are necessary to the profession, but the most important aspect—to have an idea—can't be learned. Therefore even in the age of supercomputers and CAD-CAM systems one still needs the kiss of the muse, which can only be enticed through a good relationship with the benefactress, as is well known.

On the other hand, one can attempt to learn how to turn the aforementioned kiss—should one be lucky enough to be blessed with it—into a tangible industrial product. This is a long process, requiring a bit of magic along the way. As a teacher in industrial design at the State Academy of Art and Design, I tried to develop a course of study for this process that was fueled by practical experiments. At the beginning of the semester, a group of about fifteen students of various academic years (and therefore different levels of training and experience) were given a theme which they collectively—novice or old hand—had to grapple with. These experiments were new to all the participants, and full of unknown risks and dangers. Would the muse show up? Was their idea great or useless? Is it even possible to build something like what they had in mind? How would it work? Did they have enough time to build a functional model? And if it didn't work and half the semester was over, what then? The students would try, alone and in a group, to get from a pipe dream—via sketches, drawings, research, questioning, discussions, changes, pre-visualizations, corrections, failures, complete rethinking—to a tangible, usable object that could be produced on an industrial scale. This would take them until the end of the semester—or in most cases, through the holidays up to the start of the next semester.

Every semester I would set a completely new task so as to give students an insight into the enormous range of what can be considered to be an industrial product, guaranteeing a completely new adventure. The real value of this work can obviously not be measured in the result, but in the insights each student develops into the process of creative development, adding new understanding with each new task.[46]

During the winter semester of 1990–1, I gave an assignment to design a private solar-power station. I asked the students to imagine that they lived in a detached home with a garden and they wanted, for whatever reason, to free their electricity usage from any environmental impact. For that purpose they would need to use solar energy. They were to assume the state of technology in the year 1995 for both electricity generation as well as electricity consumption. The equipment was to provide all electricity needs for the household, apart from heating, for which other technologies were more suitable. They couldn't rely on any infrastructure not currently in use at the time, and they couldn't make changes to their house. It was necessary to put a machine in the garden that was completely autonomous from anything apart from the sun, and that could generate and store electricity from sunlight: an artificial tree, so to speak. The task required the student to imagine the unimaginable: a monster in our nicely tended garden, in front of all the neighbors.

For the Yale University graphic design summer courses in Brissago, Switzerland, and for the winter semester of 1992–3 at the State Academy of Art and Design, Stuttgart, I taught an exercise in four dimensions. Using white card stock, within an area of c. 9 × 9 × 9 in. (30 × 30 × 30 cm), I asked students to develop one or more three-dimensional bodies which, when rotated 360 degrees from a defined point of origin and viewed from the side, would tell a visual story. As an example: for the students I presented a series of photographs that I had taken of the Henry Moore sculpture at Lincoln Center in New York City, where I had positioned the camera at equally spaced radial intervals around the sculpture. I have always been fascinated with objects that change form as they move or as a person moves around them, and this exercise was meant to raise awareness of visual phenomena, and to encourage an awareness of three-dimensional form.

[46] Richard Sapper, *Kontakte—Design Ausbildung*, catalog for the State Academy of Art and Design (Stuttgart, 1992).

RICHARD SAPPER

THINKPAD
(1992)
[→ PP.186–7]

The ThinkPad, and Richard's work for IBM, could easily fill a book of its own. In fact, a couple of books[47] have been written on the development of the ThinkPad, but neither of them focus exclusively on Richard's involvement, or on the design itself. Regarding the ThinkPad's design, there are a number of breakthroughs that should be mentioned. It was the first black laptop, and—thanks to independent ergonomic research commissioned by IBM—it successfully toppled DIN standards that had required computers to be beige for the previous decade. The enclosure, a simple black box, has changed proportions several times due to advances in technology, yet its principal character and concept have gone unchanged. A rubberized paint heightened the tactile experience of the outside and inside of the enclosure. The red Trackpoint at the center of the keyboard—which had to be called "magenta" to fly under the radar of IBM product managers who reserved the color red for emergency power switches—was the first of its kind and allowed users to control their cursors without taking their fingers off the keyboard. The ThinkPad had the first RGB colored screen, and the red, green, and blue IBM logo on the outside of the casing was a nod to this feature. It is Richard's most commercially successful product, having sold over one hundred million units as of January 2015.[48]

To create a product that is not functional is useless—if the design doesn't work, if it doesn't respect its function, then it is a mistake. But if a product is only functional, and it doesn't have some formal expression that awakes your interest when you look at it, and that helps in creating a human relation between you and the product, then it's not a good design. I think that a good design must have this property of awaking the interest of the person who looks at it, or keeps it in his hand, or smells it, or whatever he does with the object. This effect can create a relationship between an object and a person. The best example of this is a teddy bear. A teddy bear is also a product, but it creates a very close relationship between its owner and the product. A child who owns a teddy bear loves the teddy bear, and that's almost the same as what happens with any thing that you possess that becomes part of your life, and that is what a designer should aim for.

With the ThinkPad I wanted to create a volume that was as simple as possible and as expressive as possible. And I thought that the form of a cigar box, which at that time also corresponded to the dimensions that a laptop computer had to have, would be an expression of this. I wanted to make an object that looked like a black cigar box that on the outside shows nothing of what it is, except for the logo of the manufacturer. Then, when you open it, you would see that this is not a cigar box, but it is a computer, and you see all the complicated stuff that's inside, and that would create a surprise. And this is the basic concept of the ThinkPad. Over the years we had to update the computer many times, and it kept getting thinner and thinner with the advent of smaller and faster processors. This dematerialization continued so that the latest models are so thin and so flat that they shock you. Yet at the same time these models

---

[47] Deborah A. Dell, *ThinkPad: A Different Shade of Blue* (Indianapolis, 2000); Steve Hamm, *The Race for Perfect* (New York, 2009).
[48] Author's conversation with Tom Hardy, December 29, 2015.

maintain the ThinkPad philosophy of a square black box, albeit a version that has an extremely thin proportion and a striking appearance.

Throughout the course of his career, Richard wrote multiple essays on design, and with copies of them printed out, I ask him to discuss them with me. He explains that, sometimes, writing helps him think through certain ideas. Picking up the "Philosophy and Substance of Design," written in 1991 as the basis for a lecture, he shares the sections that interest him most.

The connection between the phenomenon of design—or rather the phenomenon of aesthetics—and the commercial success of a product, forces an emphasis on certain factors: for example, the level of novelty, a sense of sensation, fashionability, the current state of design in the product niche. In my opinion, one extremely important factor in this equation that is completely disregarded is the "desire for beauty"—a fundamentally human need. How important this need is can be seen from the tools that humanity has created for thousands of years. Even cave dwellers already understood the phenomenon of design. We measure the state of civilization of a culture by the beauty of their articles of everyday use. We can admire the beauty of such tools and objects in museums of archeology or anthropology. When we look at a 10,000-year-old tool and perceive it as beautiful, common factors such as current fashion play absolutely no role in our appreciation.

During a visit to Kyoto I once had the opportunity to take part in a local festival, which included a procession. Costumes worn were from the period around 1850. Monks, traders, aristocrats were represented. Tourists and locals lined the streets. It was therefore easy to compare clothing of people from a hundred years ago with those of today. I was shocked because the beauty, elegance, and rich coloring of the old clothing were immeasurably more beautiful than that of current clothing. I want to emphasize and explain that, in this comparison between historical products and today's beautiful products, the difference has nothing to do with technology or the conditions under which they are, or were, manufactured. The source for such quality stems from a mental attitude with which a specific project is planned.

There is an analogy I have used to underscore the futility of designers' intentions on the outcome of a product's success in the market. A baker practices his profession in order to earn money, but either he doesn't care about the quality of his bread, or he has the ambition to bake the best bread in town. Neither attitude can be a guarantee for success. A baker can bake the best bread in the city, but if next week a bread factory opens next door, he can close up shop. Admittedly, that can also happen to the baker who just wants to make money.

In my work, I could never understand the connection between the worth of a product and its commercial success. I was lucky enough to design a few products that were quite successful, but others, which I consider to be just as good, have never managed to achieve the same success. And all my customers have had the same experience. Even IBM, where I have been an adviser since 1980, makes the same many mistakes as all the others, even though they—

unlike many other companies worldwide—spend lots of money on market research and pay market research experts to find out if a product is salable or not before it comes to market. No one who throws themselves into the market knows what the end result is going to be. One can have success or failure, independent of the original intentions, because too many things can influence it.

Another question therefore poses itself: how can designers work under these circumstances? The answer to this is pretty simple. All organizations, however rational, are made up of people. And these people—not all of them, but certainly some—have an opinion, possess taste and emotions. So design unites all these irrational qualities. In all companies I have worked for, I noticed that it is specifically these psychological, emotional aspects that influence the most rational decisions in the end.

I once read in an article that the invention of the alphabet changed thinking in the Western world such that from then on, every concept, every idea had to be disassembled and then reassembled in the right sequence in order to be read and understood. This school of logical and one-dimensional thinking might have helped Western civilization to achieve world dominance, but it also attempts to switch off anything in our way of thinking that can't be clearly defined, calculated, or universally represented using numbers and letters. Our problem is that our brain is trained in this way, and we constantly try to push away the implication of those things that can't be disassembled (and there are certainly enough of those), whereas other cultures—for example, the Chinese or Japanese—that don't possess this norm can understand these concepts much better.

Ultimately, my idea of what industrial design should be adheres very closely to an architectural definition stated by the Mexican architect Luis Barragán, which, in my opinion, can be applied entirely to the situation of industrial design: "I believe in an emotional architecture. It is very important that architecture moves the mind through its beauty. If there is more than one aesthetically similar solution for a problem, then the one that gives the user the message of beauty and emotion is the true architecture." This concept can be beautifully applied to design and to all industrial products.

RUBBER CUP
(1993)
[→ P.194]

Back on the subject of teaching, we discuss what is perhaps Richard's greatest contribution to design education: the now-famous Rubber Cup competition he first organized with his students at the State Academy of Art and Design, Stuttgart.

The Rubber Cup was a "happening" that I invented for my students one semester. The idea was to make and race cars powered by rubber, so I put down certain rules that everyone had to obey: you had a rubber band that you could wind up, then release, and the car would go as far as the rubber band would propel it, but you couldn't wind it up again. As all the movement in such a race is propelled by rubber bands, the designs must be very conscious of the consumption of energy. With only a rubber band you don't have much energy at your disposal, so you must optimize everything about that vehicle in order to win. We had a race. Everybody wanted to take part in it, and it became a big thing for the students. There have been numerous Rubber Cup races over the years, and I've heard that the format has been used at other universities.

DESIGN
AND BUSINESS

Let me say that the development of new products—not only in the computer industry but everywhere—is generally compromised by the fact that those who have to pay for the development, financing the investment, do not have a lot of imagination or ideas, because people with a lot of imagination or ideas seldom choose this trade. They tend to choose something else; they usually want to be architects. Other completely different qualities are also involved, and I'm saying this without making any assessments or judgments, because I know very well that designers, who sometimes possess the qualities we talked about—imagination and courage—cannot carry out development and financing plans. They are full of ideas, which they want to implement, which means that they would go bankrupt in six months! I have had an experience which, in some ways, I consider indicative of the dangers a designer must face if he or she is not supported by people who are capable of planning and managing the outpour of ideas we mentioned before.[49]

I'm talking about a consulting service I rendered to a Swiss company; it manufactured watches and at the time I thought I had found my ideal job. On the one hand, there was a very good financial manager who had plenty of ideas, so that interesting new products could be carried out; in addition, he understood everything. On the other, there was an engineer, in charge of technical development, who I thought was absolutely skillful. If there was any technical problem I raised while developing any product, he would repeat these beautiful words: "We can do this!"

There was a problem, though, which was that the engineer never solved any problem. A few months later the company went bankrupt. From the designer's point of view, I don't know what's best: maybe facing opposition, if necessary, or reaching (through much effort) the production line with a mature feasible product. This is a common problem among Italian business people, who get carried away with excitement and are inefficient, whereas it is extremely difficult to bring a revolutionary object to the production lines in Germany, in Britain, or in the United States. The people who manage money seldom come up with something new, and when they do, the whole industrialization and marketing process is usually triggered.[50]

WEARABLE PC
(1997)
[→ P.197]

In the middle of the nineties I was convinced that the wearable PC would be the next step in the evolution of computing. No one imagined what the wearable PC was going to represent for the future of mobile computing. So we made prototypes of this device to demonstrate its capacity. We imagined a portable object, and instead of having an object on the desk—whether it be a beautiful box or an awful one—we wanted to position it in various locations about the body: we had a small screen with a microphone and an earphone that were both mounted on a pair of glasses, and then we placed a central unit in your pocket and the remote control in your hand. One problem was that people wearing such a device were going to look like monsters. This was the challenge we faced: trying not to look like monsters while using new computers. It was a very difficult yet very exciting task.

At the time I believed that the wearable PC would absorb the phone—and many other accessories and devices like agendas, alarm clocks, and calculators. The wearable PC represented a movement in computing toward miniaturization, a movement that was possible thanks to the decreasing size and increased efficiency of processing units. In this respect the Wearable PC meant a major revolution, since it involved a dimension that was completely unfamiliar.[51]

I imagined that you would be able to use this object everywhere and that this strange, composite, revolutionary object would allow so many new things. It could have been used to watch films like never before, as the screen, which was placed in front of the eye—and was only half the size of the eyeball—allowed you to see images in a life-size scale. And it was also my belief that this technology could revolutionize medical practice, as surgeons would be able to check X-rays during operations without taking their eyes off the patient. The Wearable PC would have been useful for many other professional activities, for example, mechanics that need to wire very sophisticated planes; they could save time and energy if they have the wiring diagrams before their eyes. I tried to convince IBM that they needed to do this thing for medicine, to help people who cannot function normally. But the Wearable PC never took hold the way I hoped.[52]

There wasn't very much imagination within IBM about how the Wearable PC could be marketed. They didn't think they could make money with it and so on. And after time, they didn't want to hear of it anymore.

AIDA CHAIR, AIDA TABLE & TOSCA CHAIR (1999–2007) [→ PP.202, 206, 214–15]

While Richard and I have been talking in his Milan apartment, I've been noticing some visual similarities between a nineteenth-century wooden chair that sits in the living room, and the Sapper Chair and Tosca chairs of his own design that reside in his office. The Sapper Chair carries the rolling armrests of this old wooden chair, and the Tosca has a similar construction and proportion, with the arms supported by the backrest and front legs. Richard explains that the old chair belonged to his grandmother. While his designs exploited new manufacturing techniques, he did borrow useful and elegant aspects of older archetypes, and as a result there is something familiar and comfortable to be found even in an injection-molded plastic chair like the Tosca.

The Aida and Tosca were both designed for the Italian manufacturer Magis. I ask Richard to walk me through their development.

In both cases—the Aida and the Tosca—I received a brief from Magis. I usually wait for a brief before I start working. The first chair was the Aida in polypropylene, and the second was the Tosca in air-molded polycarbonate. Aida and Tosca are the names of Italian operas, but I didn't choose these names, Magis chose them.

51–2 Interview with Maurizio Giordano, 1997.

I started these projects with a drawing. I work with one or two assistants who do some modeling on the computer, but basically my work proceeds still with materials: making models, making prototypes. I make the prototypes, and by the time I am done it is pretty difficult to distinguish my model from the actual production pieces. There were a lot of modifications, but the modifications succeed layer by layer. I go on like this until there is nothing left to change. It is difficult to know when there is nothing left to change, but you have to know it. It's important, because you could just take too long on a project, or you could not stop at the right place.

This is the traditional way of working I've always used. Recently, there is the new danger that you can rely too much on a computer drawing, and you are tempted to make something very primitive because it's so easy—then afterward it doesn't work. I still do much of my drawing by hand, in section and in perspective. Sometimes the idea is clear from the beginning, and the sketch is just there to demonstrate that idea; other times I am finding the idea in a sketch. I don't have rules about this; there are occasions where I prefer one approach, and occasions when I prefer another one. We are now in a period where we are seeing a complete change in the technology used to create three-dimensional forms. Up until now practically everything that has been manufactured has been material that is shaped by a tool with a form, or cut and bent into the desired form. But we are in the last years of these techniques because in a very short time, everything will be 3D-printed.

The Aida and Tosca share a similar center line, which is decisive for comfort. But the chairs offer very different sitting experiences. The Tosca has a much wider backrest; there is much more space in it. The Aida leans back because of the flexibility of the shape and material. The Tosca has two holes that allow the seat the breathe. Why two holes? One, two, three holes...you have to pick one! I also intended to have these holes on the Aida, but Magis abolished them. They thought it was not aesthetically correct to have holes in such a chair, and this was very stupid, because I was planning to add a textile lining on the inside of the chair, and the holes would have been the place to fix it.

I also made a table, the Aida table. The base has a structure that is made in two halves. One half is a low base, and the other half is taller with legs and wheels, and this taller half slides over the lower half of another table, so that they can stack. The top of the table has a hinge that allows it to be positioned vertically when the tables stack. This form developed from the functional requirements, I didn't have any references in mind. The Aida chair and table were imagined more for a restaurant, where they could be very useful.

They don't really produce these products in good volumes. Perhaps the Tosca sells more than the Aida, but I have never made much money there. Is a product's success determined by whether it sells or not? Well, this depends on your point of view. If you're a penny-pincher, then you are only in it for the pennies. If you are interested in something else, then it is different. For me, it is different—the most important thing is to make a good product. But to do a project like this, for a chair, is something completely different from doing a complex machine like a monitor arm. The monitor arm is a much more massive design work, and you need many more people to do it, but it has also better results.

While going through Richard's archive of personal photos, I notice that he was an avid skier, windsurfer, sailor, and even hang glider, and that in his elder years he became a rally racer. His love of motion—and forms in motion—translates into many kinetic designs such as the Tizio lamp and Sapper Monitor Arms. Once, when I bring up how, in Germany, those who acquire an excess of speeding tickets are put through some pretty thorough psychological testing, he says with a grin, "I always wanted to take that." The Zoombike, a folding bicycle, is perhaps the ultimate expression of movement and speed in Richard's work. Since the only thing he loves to discuss as much as people are technical details, I ask him to describe the workings of the Zoombike.

The Zoombike is a great technical achievement, and the result of many years of work, going back to the first folding bike I designed in 1979. Since then I had been considering how a folding bike, used in conjunction with buses and trains, could offer a transportation alternative to the automobile, and some relief to congested European cities like Milan.

The design is identical to a conventional bicycle in geometric dimensions: wheelbase, position of the handlebars, saddle, and pedals, and in the position of the rider, the pedal ratio, and mechanical efficiency. It can be folded into a package instantaneously, allowing it to be carried like a pair of skis in a bus, train, subway, or tram. It will fit into any elevator, and can be stored even in the tiniest apartment in a cupboard. At the touch of a single button, it separates into two parts that will fit in the trunk of any small car. All mechanical parts, including the drive chain, are enclosed for ease of transportation. It weighs less than a racing bike.

This combination of properties was only possible through the employment of state-of-the-art aerospace technology. While all elements that determine the riding characteristics—wheels, saddle, pedals, and handlebars—are arranged along the central axis, as with a standard bicycle, the components of the frame are placed asymmetrically left and right of it, connected with pivots so as to form a collapsible parallelogram.

The frame structure consists of extruded high-strength aluminum profiles with extremely thin walls; aluminum die-cast joints are glued into the terminals of these profiles, constituting an extremely rigid structure with minimal tolerances. The hardened surfaces of the pivots are conical, with automatic tolerance recovery. The extremely small wheel diameters are achieved using wheel suspension techniques derived from automobile manufacture.

MAY 2015, LOS ANGELES

More than a year has gone by since my last meeting with Richard. His health has been in flux and our schedules haven't lined up. But with only a few topics left to discuss, this will be our last meeting before the book goes into production. He and Dorit have come to LA from Lenovo's headquarters in Raleigh, North Carolina, and while they are here to see friends, Richard will also meet with Benjamin Pardo, design director of Knoll. I make the now-familiar drive from my office in Silver Lake to Richard's son Mathias' house in the Hollywood Hills.

TODO (2001)
[→ P.210]

While Dorit has become instrumental to Richard's professional activities in the later years of his life, helping to coordinate meetings and travel, I realize that, in addition, she has always been something of a muse to him in his work. In archival photos she frequently appears as the model user for Richard's designs, and the Nena chair [→ PP.164–5] that Richard designed for B&B Italia in 1984 was a response to Dorit's desire for chairs that could be brought out to entertain guests, then neatly put away after their departure. I remember hearing from Richard that Dorit also had something to do with the idea for the Todo cheese grater he created for Alessi, so I ask him to elaborate.

My wife, Dorit, was complaining that it took too long to grate the cheese: too many small motions. So my cheese grater is much bigger, requiring fewer motions. Maybe it was because we had grated cheese for so many years that I thought to make life simpler. It can be held more easily because of the handle on the top, instead of awkwardly from the back, as you so often have to hold them. The tilted angle of the object gives you a certain scope when you grip it because you can take it with your hands at a natural angle. When you see this object on the counter, it tells you something about what it does, and is also a dynamic form that changes as you move around it.

Compared to past Alessi projects, this one was relatively straightforward. I have always been very concerned with details, and have had to have many confrontations with engineers to get the results that I'm after. But I think something that would have made me completely mad five or ten years ago, now I am looking at with a little philosophy. It's not that I'm more tolerant with the quality of the work—oversights there still make me mad—but I'm more relaxed about the difficulties: the small problems. Naturally, I get more tired now than I did ten years ago—physically tired, that is—but my interest levels in a project, when I see something I'm enthusiastic about, haven't suffered at all.

HALLEY (2005)
[→ P.211]

The Halley is an LED lamp with an integral fan that pulls the heat away from the LEDs, which prevents them from burning out. The lamp was meant for desks in offices and houses. It has many moving parts, and as far as I know it was the first LED desk lamp in the world. It was made for a company called Lucesco that was a start-up in Silicon Valley, founded by a man who was a brilliant engineer but had no interest in sales. But he had built the company around only this product! The whole company was made for the Halley; it was highly optimistic of him. I didn't know him before, so I was not warned about his lack of interest in business, and the company didn't last long.

The lamp is asymmetrical, but the equilibrium is kept with counterweights that I have added. I used a metal sphere in one instance. The composition of the head and the sphere is like a little comet speeding by the moon, and so the lamp is named after the comet Halley. The lamp was difficult to assemble, but the huge range of movement was the next step on top of the Tizio.

It's not that I usually put on my shoes, go out, and look for new technology. If there is a new technology, you know it; you get to know it. Companies can often find interesting technologies, but it is also the designer's responsibility. Technology offers the possibility of doing something new. You know Ingo Maurer? He does all his own technology development himself. So I wasn't sleeping when LED technology came about. And naturally I was interested in it.

The Halley, because of its low energy consumption, is a much greater achievement than the original Tizio lamp. We are in a situation that is really, really critical. This environmental stuff, the heat, the climate: it is such an incredible scandal. It's a problem that has been hammered in the press for sixty years. Everybody knows about it. They've had a thousand conferences and all sorts of things have been tried, but in the end, practically nothing has been done to improve the situation. You see all those programs—all the governments here in Europe, but also in America: they have these programs to reduce CO_2 in the atmosphere, and every year it increases. Not one year did they have even partial success; every year it gets worse.

One of the most criminal operations carried out in the last hundred years was the redwood clearance in America. Eight thousand trees were felled, forests destroyed, solely to make money. But all the companies that took part in this operation have gone bankrupt. In the end not one dollar was earned and we all know very well that the destruction of the Brazilian rainforest will have the same result; nobody is going to earn anything from it.[53]

I have always, from the moment that I took on this profession, hoped to create things that create some pleasure for people, that people like to see and that they also can use. It would be like a gift for them. And that is still something to achieve; this is clear. But recently I'm thinking of other things that might be more important, and they have nothing to do with design. In the last few years, I have been convinced that we are in a historical situation that is going straight toward disaster. And individually, people do very little to help the situation. For instance, people have to pay their electricity bills, and they know what problems we are going to have in the future because of energy use, yet they are not interested in lamps that consume less energy. The Halley consumes ten percent of what a typical lamp consumes, and nobody wanted to buy it. They sold very poorly. Sure, they cost something more, but if you take a piece of paper and note how much you would save on the electricity bill, you would have made up that difference after half a year. They don't think of that!

DESIGN
AND SOCIETY

We are now living in a time in which we think we are having a lot of difficulties. I say: *think*. The designer has the advantage of having a very good insight into the functioning of the economy, and this is not always the case for other professions, because most of the activities are much more segregated than the professional activity of the designer who often has to work in all kinds of industrial sectors.

I say, we think we have a lot of difficulties. We think we could overcome these difficulties if only we knew where these difficulties and problems come from and what we could do about them. It drives me crazy to hear people saying over and over again that the bad economic situation is responsible for unemployment problems. And how something should be done now to stimulate the labor market. And how we need to boost the economy. You often hear this and similar comments. But that is total nonsense. The problems we encounter with unemployment are not caused by a bad economy; they are due to a revolution.

[53] Richard Sapper, "Philosophy and Substance of Design," lecture given at the sixth Esposizione Internazionale Mobili Ufficio (International Office Furniture Fair), September 20, 1991.

We are stuck in a revolution in the economic, social, and industrial environments. We spent decades inventing new machines and fabricating machines that replace human labor; we should therefore not be surprised to see the employment rates decrease. And we invented these machines for a good reason: so that they would do all the boring and unpleasant tasks for us.

However, we must draw the social and political consequences and reform our society in such a rightful way that the new measures not only affect the socially deprived—i.e. the unemployed—but are distributed fairly across society.

For many years, the entire middle European economy was subsisting on the export of machine tools to developing countries. It was obvious that these machine tools would begin to produce some day. We just had to adjust to it. We need to think about what actually still needs to be done. Instead of constantly thinking about redesigning useless objects we cannot sell anymore in order to make the public buy a few more, we should think about producing items that we need and that don't exist yet. There might be all sorts of objects we need; it is a question of imagination. We must ask ourselves: what is it that we actually want and need?

What we need is written in the newspaper: we have major problems in the field of environmental protection, major problems in the transport sector, in fact there are problems everywhere in our daily lives. We have sufficient intelligence and sufficient economic power to resolve these problems. All we need to do is to tackle them for once. Every industrialist has to figure out whether there is something useful he can do for society.

When studying business administration in Munich, the university had the following maxim: a businessman or an industrialist earns money as a reward in exchange for a useful service to society. This is a true principle that frequently falls into oblivion nowadays. Many of our commercial activities are not based on this principle; they are merely based on the objective to make a fast buck. It is therefore not surprising that things go wrong afterward. We should all pull ourselves together a bit and try to use our brains and our imagination to solve these problems. Design can contribute to making our life more pleasant and to ensuring an existence for all of us.[54]

SAPPER MONITOR ARM (2010) & XYZ ARM (2012) [→ PP.218–19, 221]

Over the past years of discussion with Richard, where I have planned our conversations to cover his work chronologically, on numerous occasions he has attempted to steer us into a discussion of the Sapper Monitor Arm and XYZ arm that he created for Knoll. If Richard's favorite project is the one he is "working on now," then his second favorite is the one he last designed, so I know how happy he will be finally to discuss his recent monitor arm designs, which are both here in the house. After all, he has been waiting a few years to tell me about them, and sure enough, his face lights up when I ask.

[54] Richard Sapper, "Warum macht ein Designer Design?," in *Werkzeuge für das Leben* (Göttingen, 1993).

Well, before I can talk about these projects, I must first speak a little bit about Knoll. Good clients must be willing to defend a certain state of art, and they must be willing to try something even if it has its risks. Why do some companies care to make their products beautiful? It's certainly not for money. All you have to do is look in the stores and see how successful so many terrible designs are. But I think they are interested in design because they have a general cultural interest.[55]

In the years I have worked with Knoll they have had tremendous development, especially with the internal, social setup of the company. They have had the right attitude in allowing the people in their company to create an organism that works; they have made it wonderful to work with Knoll, because they are just always helpful and interested in your work. It is the people within an organization who make it conducive to good design. Knoll is very conscious of its role in design, and it values that role.

When I worked with Knoll on my chair there was a different team in place, but for our recent work—a series of monitor arms for the workplace—I have worked very, very well together with the people at Knoll; Benjamin Pardo, Knoll's vice-president of design, and Ron Sneider, the principal engineer I work with. And then there is Andrew Cogan, the boss of Knoll. We started with the Sapper Monitor Arm, which we developed quickly and put into production, and then it was a big hit. It sold like *panini* [sandwiches], as they say in Italy. As it was so successful, we immediately started to work on another version, the XYZ, which is more complex, and moves in three axes instead of two, as the Sapper Monitor Arm does.

I have always been particularly interested in objects that move, as they are more dynamic than static objects: their form—and the user's perception of their form—changes as they move. The purpose of form in my work is the same as it is everywhere in the world: it is a language. With the monitor arms the language could fall under the title of "clarity" and "elegance." However, this is not a form that I played around with; it's not something that just happens to be like that, as it is very purposeful.

The Sapper Arm is very versatile, yet very simple. This object exists on a desk in an office, which is a busy place with not much room to spare, and so the problem is putting the monitor arm out of the way as much as it is making it accessible. You have the monitor placed on an arm that you can tilt and move in any direction from side to side, and also inward and outward if you collapse the arm in on itself. It can stow away or be present. The arm rests on a column, and it can be adjusted vertically with this knob. And you have your cable-management clips on the column as well, which allow the cables to snake down the column, adding to the form. And there are several colors: black, red, gray, with the knob always red; it's fun to design that.

In the span of a just a few years, from when we had done the basic monitor arm to when we began the XYZ, the subject of monitor arms became increasingly complex. People began to expect that they would have two screens; we found that people said, "I want to have two screens to work on: one for my shared office work and another that's more private." We heard things like that.

[55] Lance Knobel, "Richard Sapper: Breaking the Silence," in *Designer's Journal*, November 1985.

At first we began offering two monitors on the Sapper Arm with the addition of a bar across the end of the arm. But we needed a new monitor arm that was designed to carry—and move fluidly—a minimum of two screens. With the Sapper Arm, you have a simple moving structure, and so if you want to move up and down there are some adjustments to do, which is a limitation of the form. If you want to move it fluidly up and around, it's not the right form for that. So I chose a completely different principle for the XYZ, which is the inclusion of a gas cylinder, and a very different type of joint that corresponds to it. But when the object gets more complex, as the XYZ is, I try to maintain the clarity of the form.

I always have many aesthetic references, but I can't easily put these into words. I have many favorite sculptors, but one of them is certainly Henry Moore. I just love his forms; of all the sculptors that I enjoy, he is perhaps the closest to my view. But I like to look at a thousand things; I am very keen on anything that is interesting to see. For instance, I have a picture of a whale's tail on my wall because I think it is very interesting. But I wouldn't say that my work is directly related to this or that piece of inspiration, or that the monitor arms are directly associated with the whale's tail.

In Milan, Richard has a book on Alexander Calder, who might be the obvious artistic reference for his kinetic works. But the mention of Henry Moore—whose Lincoln Center sculpture he used as the basis of his Yale summer courses in Brissago—is enlightening. It makes me realize that, beyond their actual movement, the monitor arms Richard designed for Knoll (along with so much of his other work) are principally works of visual articulation through the interplay of elements. I ask if he agrees—and I get a smile and a nod.

Richard is a family man; this can be seen in his strong connection to his ancestry, to his loyalty to and evident love of Dorit, and his closeness to his children and grandchildren. Perhaps the humanity that comes across in his work owes something to the fact that he has always organized his professional activity around his family and within his many homes. Several times in our conversations, Richard has voiced concern over the future of the environment, each time asking himself how he would explain this disaster to his children and grandchildren, as if he had personally failed them. His concern for posterity in design seems to come as much from the spiritual inheritance he received from the ancestors that were so dear to him as it does from his concern about his own family's future. In the final moments of our last meeting I ask Richard to describe how he organized his practice to maintain closeness with his personal life and interests.

I have never needed a big design office. The way I've worked has never changed; the objects I do, I do with very few people. What I like about our profession is designing. If I had other people working with me, in the end these people would do what I like to do. I don't like directing people, dealing with contracts, handling PR activities, or being constantly on the phone. I want to design objects. If I need someone, I get this person. I get help from someone who knows what I want from him or her at a certain point. I have three assistants now, but I don't work with them all the time. They work part-time, and usually from their own offices. They mainly help with 3D modeling. I have been using 3D modeling since the earliest days of the software, and while I know this software, I don't operate it well, and have always relied on assistants for this.

Of course, I have my own office for all the administrative tasks. I would like to be able to decline tasks I don't like, but this is only possible to a certain degree. I have no idea how many hours I spend talking on the phone; it is ridiculous, but that's how it is. Even processing mail is very time-consuming. But I don't think that things would be better with a big studio and employees, because I would have to coordinate everything and that would be time-consuming, too.

Design is always a collaborative process with the client, but by doing the design myself at least I control this process.

PART III

CHRONOLOGY

1932

RICHARD FRANK SAPPER IS BORN
IN MUNICH, GERMANY
May 30

1938

RICHARD AS A BOY
Germany

Early 1950s

RICHARD AS A STUDENT
Munich, Germany

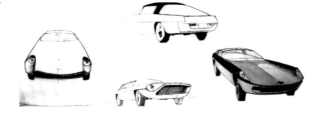

1955

SKETCHES FOR AUTOMOBILE DESIGNS
Germany

1956

RICHARD GRADUATES WITH
A DEGREE IN BUSINESS FROM THE
UNIVERSITY OF MUNICH
Germany

1956

REARVIEW MIRROR
Mercedes 300 SL Roadster
Daimler-Benz
Germany

[← P.56]

MODISCH—MODERN: EIN PROBLEM
DER INDUSTRIELLEN FORMGEBUNG
Essay by Richard Sapper
Graphik: Werbung und Formgebung
Issue no. 5

1957

TELEPHONE WITH
PUSH-BUTTON KEYS
Mix & Genest
Germany

1957

RICHARD WITH HIS PARENTS
Lake Constance, Germany

1958

MOPED IMN (SKETCH)
with Alberto Rosselli
IMN
Italy

[← P.59]

1958

MODEL FOR DOOR-HANDLE DESIGN
with Gianfranco Frattini
Italy

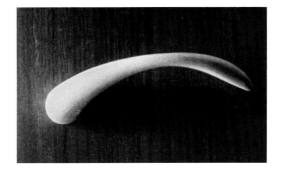

1958

CEILING LAMP
La Rinascente
Italy

1958

TROPHY FOR SPORTS EVENTS
La Rinascente
Italy

1958

COFFEE GRINDER
with Marco Zanuso
Girmi
Italy

1959

TRANSMASTER 7
Transistor radio
La Rinascente
Italy

1959

HAIR DRYER
La Rinascente
Italy

[← P.59]

1959

RICHARD MEETS DORIT POLZ
Milan, Italy

Early 1960s

RICHARD WORKING AT HIS DESK
AT STUDIO ZANUSO
Milan, Italy

1960

TABLE LAMP
Prototype
Italy

1960

SCHOOL DESK
with Marco Zanuso
Milan City Council
Italy

1960

MODEL SHIP STRUCTURE
FOR CHILDREN'S PLAYGROUND
with Marco Zanuso
Milan City Council
Italy

1960

STATIC
Table clock
Lorenz, Italy

– Winner, Compasso d'Oro, 1960

[← P.60]

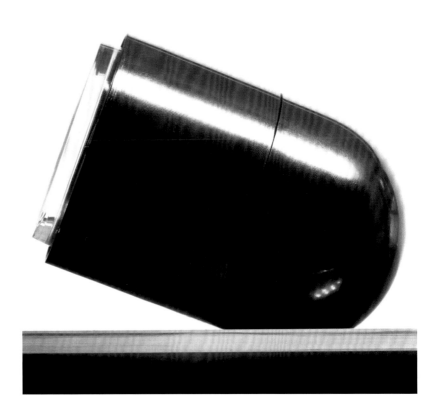

1960

HELIOS
Wall clock
Lorenz
Italy

1961

MOPED
Hercules
Germany

1961

TRADE FAIR STAND FOR PIRELLI
with Marco Zanuso and Pino Tovaglia
Milan, Italy

1962

MATCH
Transistor radio
Telefunken
Germany

1962

INDUSTRIAL SEWING MACHINE
with Marco Zanuso
Necchi
Italy

1962

NECCHI 564
Sewing machine
with Marco Zanuso
Necchi
Italy

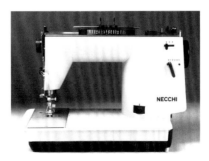

1962

DONEY
Television
with Marco Zanuso
Brionvega
Italy

– Winner, Compasso d'Oro, 1962
– Included in the permanent design
collection at the Museum of Modern
Art, New York

1963

ANTARES
Television
Brionvega
Italy

1963

TS 502
Radio
with Marco Zanuso
Brionvega
Italy

– Gold Medal, BIO 2, Ljubljana, 1966
– Bundespreis, "Die Gute Form," 1969
– Included in the permanent design
collection at the Museum of Modern
Art, New York

[← P.60]

1963

ALFA ROMEO SPORT
Sports car
with Marco Zanuso
Alfa Romeo
Italy

<u>1963</u>

LAMBDA
Sheet-metal chair
with Marco Zanuso
Gavina
Italy

– Included in the permanent design
collection at the Museum of Modern
Art, New York

[← P.62]

RICHARD SAPPER

1963

RICHARD AND DORIT ARE MARRIED
Stuttgart, Germany
January 16

1963

RICHARD AND DORIT'S FIRST CHILD
CAROLA IS BORN

1964

ALFA ROMEO SPORT
Sports car
with Marco Zanuso
Alfa Romeo
Italy

1964

ALGOL
Portable TV set
with Marco Zanuso
Brionvega
Italy

– Included in the permanent design
collection at the Museum of Modern
Art, New York

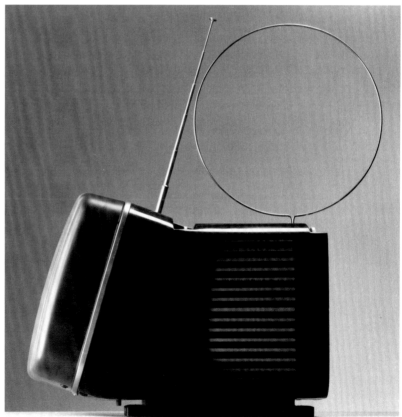

1964

K 1340
Polyethylene children's chair
with Marco Zanuso
Kartell
Italy

– Winner, Compasso d'Oro, 1964
– Gold Medal, Triennale XIII, 1964
– Grand Prix, International
Plastics Exhibition, London, 1965
– Included in the permanent design
collection at the Museum of Modern
Art, New York

[← P.63]

ELECTRONIC MINI COMPUTER
with Marco Zanuso
Olivetti
Italy

1964

RICHARD IN A SKI RACE
Kitzbühel, Austria

1964

RICHARD AND DORIT, WITH
DAUGHTER CAROLA IN THE CRIB,
ON THE TERRACE OF RICHARD'S
PARENTS' HOUSE
Stuttgart, Germany

1964

TELEVISION
16" Television set
Telefunken
Germany

1964

NECCHI 400
Industrial sewing machine
with Mark Zanuso
Necchi
Italy

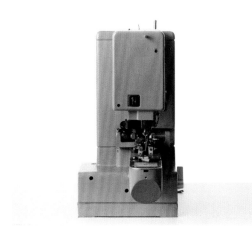

1964

KNIFE SHARPENER
with Marco Zanuso
Necchi
Italy

– Included in the permanent design
collection at the Museum of Modern
Art, New York

1964

TRANSISTOR RADIO
Telefunken
Germany

1965

RR 127
Radio
with Marco Zanuso
Brionvega
Italy

1965

GRILLO
Telephone
with Marco Zanuso
Siemens Italtel
Germany/Italy

– Winner, Compasso d'Oro, 1967
– Gold Medal, BIO 3, Ljubljana, 1968
– Included in the permanent design
collection at the Museum of Modern
Art, New York

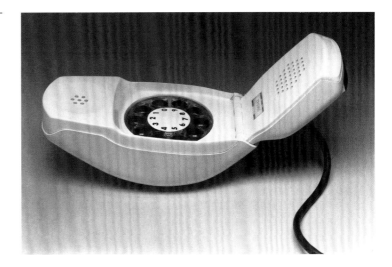

1965

RICHARD AND MARCO ZANUSO
WITH THE GRILLO TELEPHONE
Milan, Italy

1965

RICHARD SAILING A FINN
Lake Como, Italy

1966

ALCIONE
Television
Brionvega
Italy

1966

RICHARD AND DORIT'S SECOND
CHILD MATHIAS IS BORN

1967

REMOTE CONTROL
with Marco Zanuso
Brionvega
Italy

This was one of the first television
remote controls. It only controlled
the power.

1967

RICHARD
Scotland, UK

1968

ADVANCED TECHNOLOGIES
EXHIBITION STAND
with William Plumb and Pio Manzú
Triennale XIV
Milan, Italy

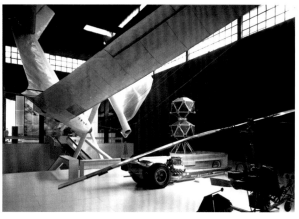

1968

STUDY FOR AUTOMOBILE BODY
Carrozzeria Touring
Italy

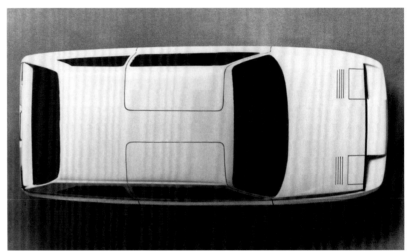

1968

YADES
Television
with Marco Zanuso
Brionvega
Italy

1969

SINTES
Prefabricated kitchen-bathroom module
with Luigi Caramella and Gianmaria Beretta
Sintes
Italy

1969

PREFAB—UNA CELLA BAGNO-CUCINA
Domus
Issue no. 471, February

1969

RICHARD WITH DAUGHTER CAROLA
AND SON MATHIAS ON LAKE COMO
Italy

1969

PAGER
Zetrop Spa
Italy

The pager displayed number
sequences that corresponded
to preprogrammed contacts.

– Prize Premio, SMAU, 1969

1970

BLACK
Television set
with Marco Zanuso
Brionvega
Italy

– Honourable Mention, BIO 5,
Ljubljana, 1973
– Included in the permanent design
collection at the Museum of Modern
Art, New York

1970

MANGIANASTRI RM305
Cassette recorder
with Marco Zanuso
Brionvega
Italy

1970

FD 1102
Wired radio device
with Marco Zanuso
Brionvega
Italy

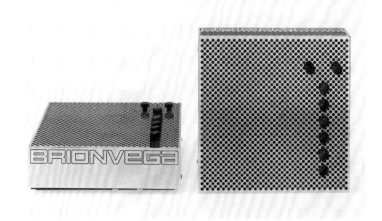

1971

TANTALO
Table clock
Artemide
Italy

[← P.66]

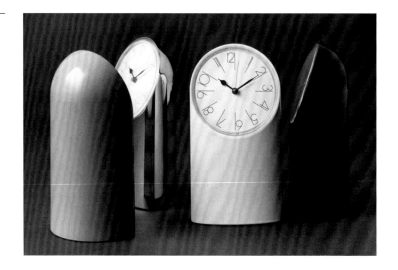

1971

SANDWICH
Alarm clock
Ritz-Italora
Italy

To stop the alarm, the user had to
press the outer elements inwards.
The name was derived from this
"sandwich" of components.

1971

ROCKET
Digital clock
Ritz-Italora
Italy

– Gold Medal, BIO 5, Ljubljana, 1973

1971

WALL CLOCK
Prototype
Ritz-Italora
Italy

1971

MINITIMER
Kitchen timer
Ritz-Italora
Italy

– Included in the permanent design
collection at the Museum of Modern
Art, New York

1971

RICHARD AND DORIT'S THIRD CHILD
CORNELIA IS BORN

1972

ITALY: THE NEW DOMESTIC LANDSCAPE
Exhibition catalog
Cover artwork by Emilo Ambasz
Museum of Modern Art, New York

Featuring the Mobile Housing Unit,
designed by Richard and Marco Zanuso.

[← P.64]

1972

MOBILE HOUSING UNIT
Site-specific installation for *Italy: The New Domestic Landscape* exhibition
with Marco Zanuso
Museum of Modern Art
New York, USA

[← P.63]

1972

TIZIO
Desk lamp
Artemide
Italy

– Grand Prix, Triennale XV, 1974
– Gold Medal, Triennale XV, 1974
– Gold Medal, BIO 9, Ljubljana, 1981
– Included in the permanent design
collection at the Museum of Modern
Art, New York

[← P.66]

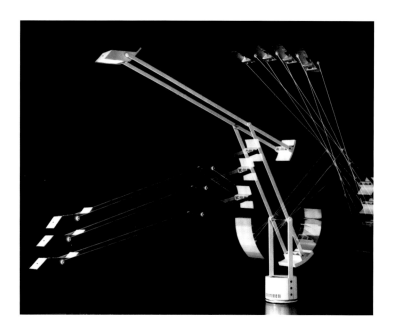

1972

REMOTE CONTROL
with Marco Zanuso
Brionvega
Italy

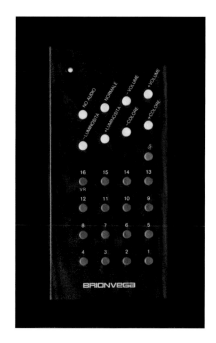

1972

CITY TRAFFIC STUDY FOR MILAN
Competition entry for "Milano invece
di Milano," awarded by ADI (Associazione
Disegno Industriale)
with Gae Aulenti
Italy

[← P.72]

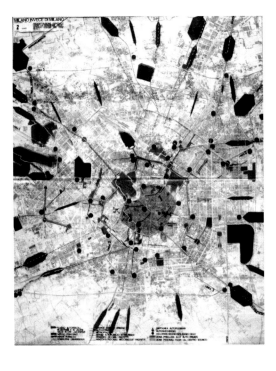

1972

HASTIL
Fountain pen
with Marco Zanuso
Aurora
Italy

– Included in the permanent design
collection at the Museum of Modern
Art, New York

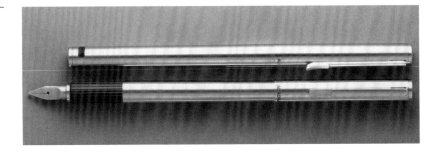

1972

POLIVALENTE
Kitchen extractor fan
with Marco Zanuso
Vortice
Italy

1973

RICHARD WITH HIS THREE CHILDREN
ON THE LAWN AT THE SAPPER FAMILY
RESIDENCE
Lake Como, Italy

1973

RICHARD WITH SON MATHIAS
AND DAUGHTER CORNELIA
Corsica

1974

SURPRISE BOX
Kitchen unit
with Luca Meda and Michele Casalucci
Unifor
Italy

1974

X 126 SOFTNOSE
Experimental automobile prototype
FIAT
Italy

The X 126 Softnose was the first car
conceived with a full-body plastic bumper
to protect against low-impact collisions.

[← P.65]

1974

GENIA
Modular bookshelf system
B&B Italia
Italy

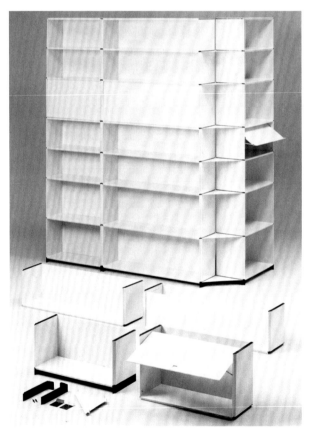

1975

MISURA
Office furniture system
with Luca Meda and Michele Casalucci
Unifor
Italy

1975

CONCETTO 101
Hi-Fi stereo system
with Marco Zanuso
Brionvega
Italy

1976

RICHARD AND DORIT AT A RECEPTION
Milan, Italy

<u>1976</u>

MICROSPLIT 520
Stopwatch
Heuer
Switzerland

– Included in the permanent design
collection at the Museum of Modern
Art, New York

[← P.67]

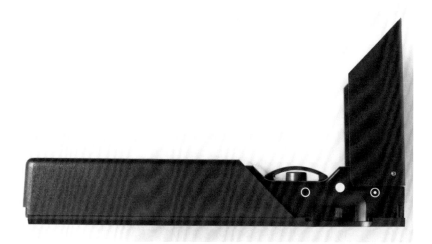

RICHARD SAPPER

1976

PRIVATE BUS
Armored private bus for Silvio Berlusconi
FIAT
Italy

1976

PLICO
Foldable beverage trolley
Bilumen
Italy

FOLDING BICYCLE
Batavus
The Netherlands

AERMEC
Air-conditioning unit
Riello
Italy

MICROSPLIT 370
Wrist stopwatch
Heuer
Switzerland

1977

MICROSPLIT 320
Stopwatch
Heuer
Switzerland

1977

PM10
Pulse meter
Heuer
Switzerland

1978

RICHARD ON THE LAWN
Lake Como, Italy

9090
Espresso coffee maker
Alessi
Italy

– Winner, Compasso d'Oro, 1979
– Honorable Mention, BIO 9,
Ljubljana, 1981
– Included in the permanent design
collection at the Museum of Modern
Art, New York

[← P.69]

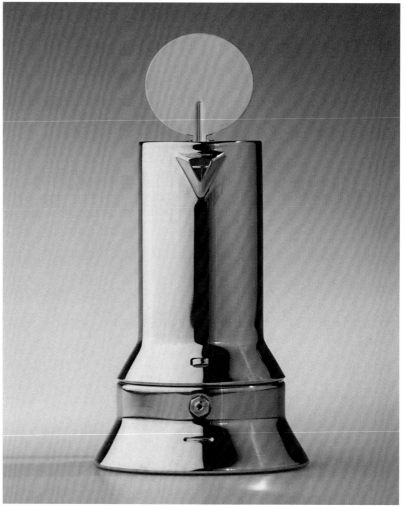

1978

AIR-CONDITIONING UNIT
Riello
Italy

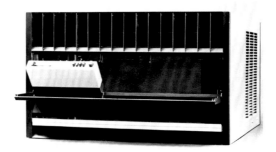

1978

RICHARD SKETCHING IN HIS OFFICE
Milan, Italy

1978

RICHARD WITH SON MATHIAS
AND DAUGHTER CORNELIA
Santa Cruz, California, USA

1978

2000 MULTIMETER AND 2000
VOM PROBE
Digital multimeter
Heuer
Switzerland

1979

RICHARD WITH SON MATHIAS
IN HIS OFFICE
Milan, Italy

1979

STUDY FOR URBAN TRANSIT:
[RIGHT AND OPPOSITE]
MOVING WALKWAY, BUS FOR BICYCLE,
BICYCLE UMBRELLA, FOLDING SCOOTER
Triennale XVI
Milan, Italy

[← P.72]

RICHARD SAPPER

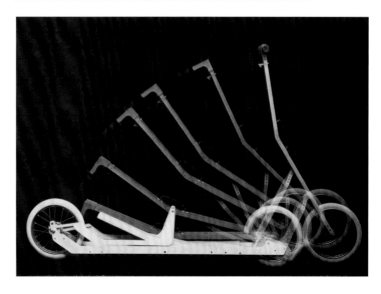

1979

SAPPER CHAIR
Executive office chairs and seating
system
Knoll
USA

– Prize Premio, SMAU, 1981
– Bundespreis "Die gute Form," 1982

[← P.70]

1979

RICHARD STUDYING COOKWARE
Point, Vienne, France

Point, VIENNE, Giugno '79.

Late 1970s

MEETING AT B&B ITALIA
From left to right: Piero Ambrogio
Busnelli, Richard, Mario Bellini,
Gae Aulenti, and Vico Magistretti
Milan, Italy

1979

VK 118 A
Vacuum cleaner
Vorwerk
Germany

RICHARD IS HIRED AS IBM'S
INDUSTRIAL DESIGN CONSULTANT

Richard is hired to replace Eliot Noyes,
who had been IBM's design consultant
from 1957 until his death in July 1977.

1980

PEOPLE AND PROJECTS
Article by George Finley
I.D.
May/June

Announcement of Richard's new role
as IBM's industrial design consultant.

[← P.74]

1980

ESCARGOT
Kitchen timer
Terraillon
France

1980

RICHARD AND DORIT SAILING
ON A TORNADO CATAMARAN
Lake Como, Italy
[RIGHT AND OPPOSITE]

RICHARD PREPARING FOR
A SAILING TRIP
[OPPOSITE BOTTOM]

IBM UPRIGHT TYPEWRITER
Prototype
IBM
USA

[← P.75]

1981

RICHARD AND FRIENDS SKIING
Mont Blanc, the Graian Alps

1981

SPAGHETTI FORK
Prototype created during the design
conference "Essen und Ritual"
organized by Alessi
Berlin, Germany

[← P.77]

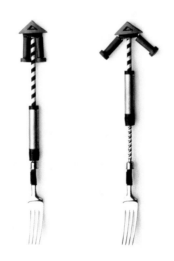

1981

SAPPER RESIDENCE
Designed by Marco Zanuso
Lake Como, Italy

The house was designed in dialog
with Dorit and Richard and features
a workshop area for Richard. This
house—and its lawn—was the location
for many of Richard's meetings and
workshops with clients.

1982

SOLDIER ROBOT
Milan, Italy

Richard designed this robot for his
children, recycling the mechanism
of an existing toy.

<u>1982</u>

4060
Coffee and tea set
Alessi
Italy

The 4060 was developed specifically
for the hospitality industry.

1982

RICHARD IN A WIND GLIDER
Designed by Carlo Ferrarin and Livio Sonzio
Caproni Vizzola
Italy

1982

DESIGN UND DESIGNER—WOZU
EIGENTLICH? WARUM MUß
DER ARBEITGEBERGESCHMACK
AKZEPTIERT WERDEN?
Essay by Richard Sapper
Bit—Büro und Informationstechnik
Issue no. 11, November

1983

RICHARD WITH HIS DOG BEPA
Lake Como, Italy

1983

RICHARD WITH MATHIAS
AND CORNELIA
Greece

1983

RICHARD AND INSTRUCTOR
ON A HANG GLIDER
Saint Moritz, Switzerland

1983

RICHARD WITH EILA HERSHON
New York, USA

In 1983, Eila Hershon and Robert Guerra
made a six-part documentary series called
By Design, which profiled Richard, Elliott
Erwitt, Milton Glaser, Karl Lagerfeld,
Benjamin and Jane Thompson, and Massimo
and Lella Vignelli. The series was shown
on television stations internationally.

<u>1983</u>

UN FUTURO POSSIBILE
Contribution to a panel discussion
with Ernesto Gismondi, Vico Magistretti,
Mario Bellini, Richard Sapper, Gae Aulenti,
Cini Boeri, Ettore Sottsass, and Michele
De Lucchi during the Salone del Mobile
Milan, Italy

<u>1983</u>

9091
Tea kettle
Alessi
Italy

[← P.79]

1984

KNOLL'S NEW GANG IN TOWN
Article by Deyan Sudjic
Blueprint
Issue no.7

An article featuring Richard and other
Knoll designers: Cini Boeri, Niels
Diffrient, and Ettore Sottsass.

Early 1980s

RICHARD AND ALBERTO ALESSI
A meeting in the offices of Alessi to
review the 9090 and 4060
Crusinallo, Italy
[RIGHT]

A walk in Orta San Giulio,
Crusinallo, Italy
[OPPOSITE]

1984

NENA
Folding armchair
B&B Italia
Italy

[← P.90]

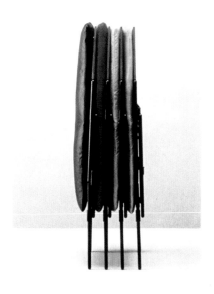

RICHARD SAPPER

1984

RICHARD PRESENTS THE TIZIO LAMP
ON ITALIAN TELEVISION
Milan, Italy

1985

THE TIZIO; STATUS ICON OF THE '80s
Article by Patricia Leigh Brown
The Philadelphia Enquirer
March 17

SUNDAY, MARCH 17, 1985 - THE PHILADELPHIA

The Tizio: Status icon of the '80s

By Patricia Leigh Brown
Inquirer Staff Writer

NEW YORK — When the Tizio lamp made its debut in 1972, people would trundle over to the strange-looking black object and ask, "Now what does one do with this?" After all, it didn't really look like a lamp. It looked a bit like a miniature abstract metal giraffe grazing at a watering hole.

But here's the Tizio — "the status icon of the '80s, replacing the Barcelona chair as the design must-have," as Metropolitan Home magazine recently cooed. Like pod people, the Tizio is everywhere. There are Tizios on Johnny Carson's L.A. pad and Tizios on certain Estee Lauder makeup counters. The Tizio lends its image to Final Net hair spray commercials and Herman Miller furniture ads. It was prominently displayed on Morgan Fairchild's desk in *Paper Dolls* and can still be seen with Angela Lansbury in *Murder, She Wrote*. It's even on the cover of the new book *French Style* (the lamp is Italian, but never mind).

To Tizio owner Christopher Wilk, decorative-arts curator at the Brooklyn Museum, the Tizio is "the lamp of our times." He calls it "wonderfully functional and beautiful. It has tremendous presence as an object."

So what does Richard Sapper, the man who designed the Tizio, think of

(See LAMP on 8-K)

Special to The Inquirer / SUSAN MAY TELL

Designer Richard Sapper, with a floor version of the Tizio lamp

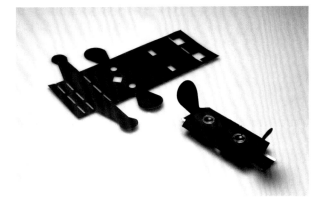

<u>1985</u>

STEREO SLIDE VIEWER
Trediland
Italy

This folded cardboard structure was
used to view individual slides.

<u>1985</u>

RICHARD SAPPER:
BREAKING THE SILENCE
Article by Lance Knobel
Designers' Journal
November

<u>1985–96</u>

RICHARD TEACHES IN THE YALE SUMMER
PROGRAM IN GRAPHIC DESIGN
Brissago, Switzerland

[← P.81]

MOD. 5140
Convertible personal computer
with Colleen Sweeney
IBM
USA

The MOD. 5140 was IBM's first laptop
computer.

– Prize Premio, SMAU, 1986
– IF Product Design Award, 1988

[← P.76]

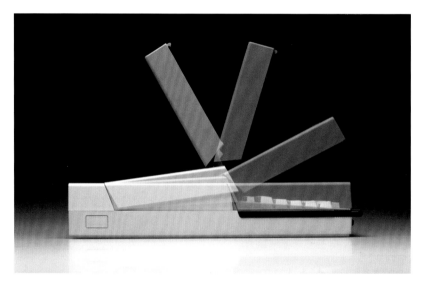

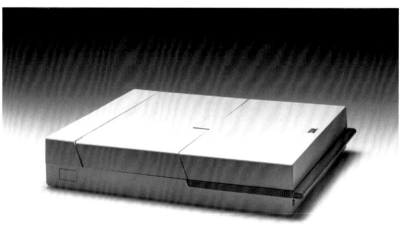

1985

RICHARD, WITH HIS HAND
IN THE "MOUTH" OF THE MOD. 5140
Boca Raton, Florida

The MOD. 5140 was developed
in the IBM Design Center in Boca Raton,
Florida, an area notoriously infested
with alligators. In profile, the MOD. 5140
bears a resemblance to an alligator's head,
and paper emitting from its rear-mounted
printer recalls an alligator's tail.

[← P.76]

1986

RICHARD SAPPER:
PC CONVERTABLE IBM
Article by Marco Romanelli
Domus
Issue no. 674, July/August

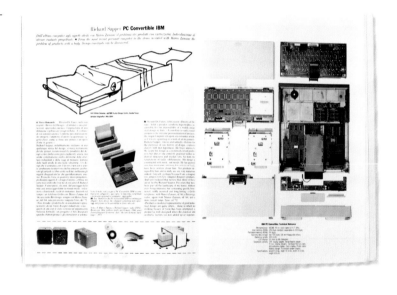

1986

ARETUSA
Suspension lamp
Artemide
Italy

This lamp was developed for the
Rumpus Room installation at the
Triennale XVII in Milan.

1986

RUMPUS ROOM
Installation for the Triennale XVII
Milan, Italy

The Rumpus Room was an experimental
family and hobby room incorporated
into a single piece of furniture. Lighting,
tools, and games hung from ropes
connected to an overhead structure.
Each item could be lowered individually.

1986

FROM 9 TO 5
Office furniture system
Castelli
Italy

– Winner, Compasso D'Oro, 1987

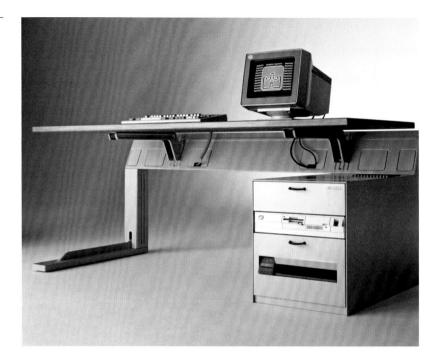

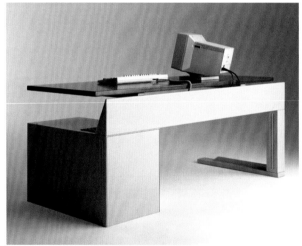

1986

IBM'S ROAD MACHINE
Article by Paul Freiberger
PC World
Issue no. 8, August

RICHARD SAPPER

1986

TELEPHONE BOOTH
Deutsche Bundespost
Germany

1986

RICHARD SAPPER: BATTERIA
DA CUCINA, OFFICINA ALESSI
Article by Marco Romanelli
Domus
Issue no. 676, October

1986

LA CINTURA DI ORIONE
Cookware set
Alessi
Italy

[← P.80]

RICHARD SAPPER

1987

LA CUCINA ALESSI
by Alberto Alessi and Alberto Gozzi
Artwork by Milton Glaser
Longanesi, Milan

[THIS EDITION]
Econ Verlag, Düsseldorf, 1988

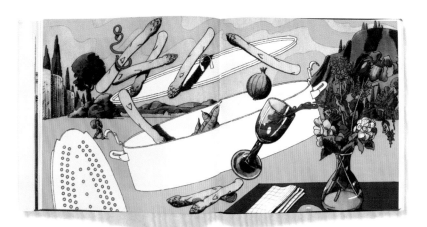

1987

RICHARD WORKING IN HIS OFFICE
Baden-Baden, Germany

Mid-1980s

RICHARD IN HIS OFFICE
Milan, Italy

<u>1987</u>

TIZIO
Lecture during Westweek
Pacific Design Center
Los Angeles, USA

<u>1987</u>

MADDALENA DE PADOVA, RICHARD
AND DORIT
Milan, Italy

<u>1987</u>

PS/2 MODEL 30
Personal computer
IBM
USA

<u>1987</u>

THE DESIGN PROCESS
Essay by Richard Sapper
Pacific Design Center News
May

1988

RICHARD SAPPER:
40 PROGETTI DI DESIGN
by Dorit Sapper, Donata Cocchi,
and Roberto Sambonet
with the support of Commune di Milano
Artemide-Litech, Milan

[← P.70]

1988

ARGO
Track-lighting system
Artemide-Litech
Italy

The low-voltage track-lighting system
had integrated adapters and the
spotlights could be tilted and pointed
in all directions.

– IF Product Design Award, 1990

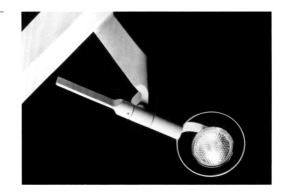

1988

SAPPER, 40 PROGETTI DI DESIGN
1958–88
Traveling exhibition
Milan, Barcelona, Paris, New York

1988

SYSTEM 26
Executive office chairs and seating
system
Comforto
Germany

1988

URIURI
Wrist watch
Alessi
Italy

1989

SAPPER RESIDENCE
Designed by Marco Zanuso
Via Beretta, Milan, Italy

This apartment was the last time that
Richard would work with Marco Zanuso
before his death in 2001. The home features
an office that functioned as Richard's
principal working environment. It is still
Dorit's primary residence.

1989

SECRETAIRE
Cabinet-workstation
with Mathias Sapper
Unifor
Italy

The height of the work surface
could be adjusted electronically,
allowing the user to work from
seated or standing positions.

– IF Product Design Award, 1990

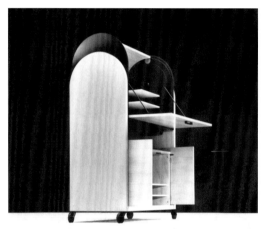

Late 1980s

RICHARD HITTING A TENNIS BALL
FOR HIS DOG BEPA
Lake Como, Italy

Late 1980s

RICHARD WITH HIS STUDENTS
Yale Summer Program
Brissago, Switzerland

[← P.81]

1990

TIZIO PLUS
Desk lamp
Artemide
Italy

This version of the lamp offered a head
that tilted on two axes, allowing light
to be more precisely directed. This feature
was planned for the original design but was
postponed because it was considered too
complicated for production.

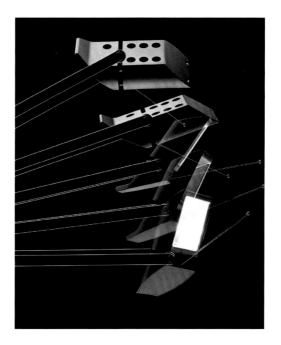

1990

SAPPER RESIDENCE
Los Angeles

Richard and Dorit purchased their house in
the Hollywood Hills area of Los Angeles, as
their son Mathias had moved to the city to
study film. Richard worked from the house
and hosted meetings with clients on many
of his trips to the US.

1990

RICHARD AND KAZUHIKO
YAMAZAKI OF IBM
Richard presents the first ThinkPad
model at his home office
Milan, Italy

1991

POWER TRANSMISSION SYSTEM
Hurth-Axle
Italy

This modular axle system was designed
for a range of earth-moving machinery
of varying types and sizes.

– Winner, Compasso d'Oro, 1991

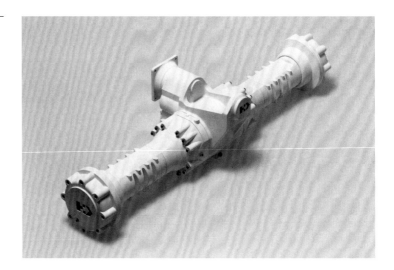

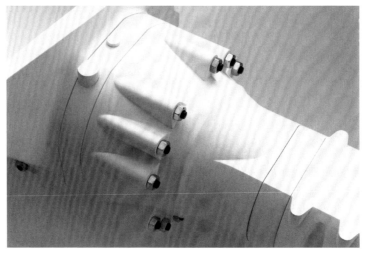

<u>1991</u>

SWATH
Study for passenger ship
with gambling facilities
Cosulich
Italy

Employing SWATH technology for
a large-scale passenger ship, this design
was intended to eliminate pitching
and rolling for waves as large as 23 ft.
(7 m) high.

<u>1991</u>

RICHARD IN HIS OFFICE WITH
A MODEL OF THE SWATH
Milan, Italy

<u>1991</u>

FILOSOFIA E CONTENUTO NEL DESIGN
Lecture during the conference "The
Meaning of Design, Design Management
and Patent Rights within the Context of
the European Market"
EIMU (Esposizione Internazionale Mobili
Ufficio)
Milan, Italy

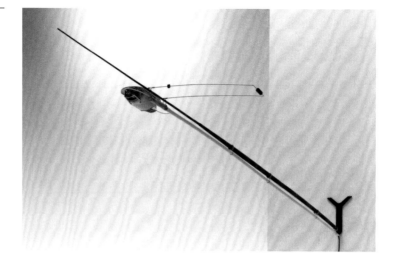

1991

ASTARTE
Wall-mounted lighting
Artemide
Italy

1991

PS NOTEBOOK
Laptop computer
with Kazuhiko Yamazaki
IBM
USA

1991

IBM PS55
with Kazuhiko Yamazaki
IBM
USA

A precursor to the ThinkPad laptop

1991

WHERE GOD LIVES: AN INTERVIEW
WITH RICHARD SAPPER
Article by Chee Pearlman
I.D.
May/June

1991–2

PERSONALITY STUDIES
Model
IBM
USA

Richard's "personality studies" were
a series of abstract formal models
intended to offer guidance to IBM
designers as they worked on mainframe
computers, servers, and desktop
computers. They included linear fan
vents, bold rectilinear forms,
and curved touch points, which all
became hallmark IBM, and now Lenovo,
design features.

[← P.77]

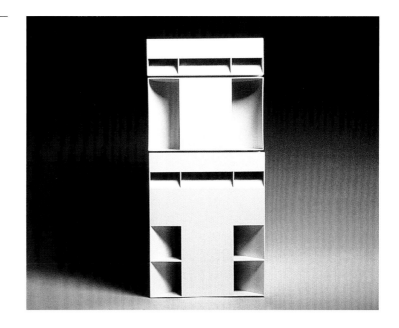

1992

THINKPAD 700T
IBM
USA

The 700T had an articulating cover
that could be used as a tablet with
a pen. It was the first IBM product
with the ThinkPad name. The name
ThinkPad was derived from an IBM
note pad with the word "Think" on
its cover.

1992

THINKPAD 700C
with Kaz Yamazaki
IBM
USA

– IF Product Design Award, 1993

[← P.83]

RICHARD SAPPER

PS/1 MODEL 111
Personal computer
with Joe Kasinski
IBM
USA

The PS/1 MODEL 111 was one of IBM's
early consumer-oriented products.

1992

BANDUNG
Teapot
Alessi
Italy

Inspired by an antique baroque Dutch
teapot, this product allowed tea to be
steeped in a horizontal position. In the
vertical position, the tea leaves were
isolated from the freshly-brewed tea
(stopping the tea from over-steeping).

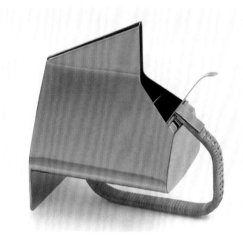

1992

IST DESIGN ÜBERHAUPT LEHRBAR?
Essay by Richard Sapper
Kontakte—Design Ausbildung
Edition Cantz, Stuttgart

1992

LEAPFROG
Tablet computer prototype
with Sam Lucente
IBM
USA

– Winner, Compasso d'Oro, 1994

1992

RICHARD RECEIVES THE LUCKY STRIKE
DESIGNER AWARD

WARUM MACHT EIN DESIGNER DESIGN?
Acceptance speech during the presentation
of the Raymond Loewy Lucky Strike
Designer Award
First published in *Design Report*
Issue no. 22, November

1993

RICHARD SAPPER:
WERKZEUGE FÜR DAS LEBEN
by Uta Brandes
Design by Paul Rand
Steidl, Göttingen

VERKEHRSFORMEN—DIE
MAILÄNDER VERKEHRSSTUDIE
Essay by Richard Sapper
Werkzeuge für das Leben
Steidl, Göttingen

[← P.70]

1993

RICHARD SAPPER DESIGN
Exhibition at the Museum für
Angewandte Kunst
Poster design by Paul Rand
Hamburg, Germany

1993

CODE NAME: LEAPFROG
Article by Julie Trelstad
I.D.
May/June

1993

THE ART OF THE POSSIBLE
Essay by Richard Sapper
Design Review
Issue no. 7, Volume 2

1993

RICHARD SAPPER DESIGN
Exhibition at the Museum für
Angewandte Kunst
Köln, Germany

1993

MARCO ZANUSO AND RICHARD SAPPER:
SELECTIONS FROM THE DESIGN
COLLECTION
Exhibition at the Museum of Modern Art,
New York, USA

RICHARD SAPPER DESIGN
Exhibition catalog
Edited by Gabriele Lueg
Museum für Angewandte Kunst
Köln, Germany

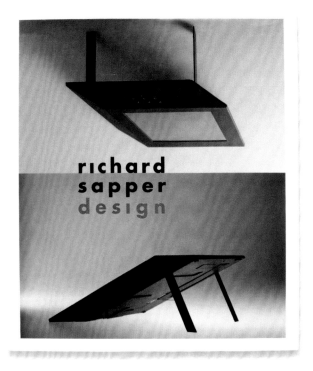

1994

THINKPAD 755C
IBM
USA

The back of the screen could be removed,
converting the main display into a
translucent screen that could be placed on
an overhead projector for presentations.

1994

THINKPAD 360P
IBM
USA

Laptop with a flip screen and pen

1994

LEAPFROG COMPUTER
Article by Marco Romanelli
Domus
Issue no. 757, February

1994

RICHARD SAPPER
Exhibition in Arc en rêve
Bordeaux, France

1995

RS01
Cutlery set
Alessi
Italy

1995

THINKPAD 701C
with Sam Lucente, John Karidis,
and Robert Tennant
IBM
USA

The ThinkPad 701C featured a
foldable keyboard, allowing for the
use of a standard-size keyboard on
a more compact laptop body.

– IF Product Design Award, 1996
– Included in the permanent design
collection at the Museum of Modern
Art, New York

1995

RUBBER CUP (POSTER)
Student competition organized by Richard
Stuttgart State Academy of Art and Design
Germany

[← P.85]

1995

THINKPAD 755CDV
IBM
USA

The back of the screen could be
removed, converting the main display
into a translucent screen that could
be placed on an overhead projector
for presentations.

1995

THINKPAD PC110
IBM
USA

The IBM PC110 was about the size
of a paperback book and was so small
that it was considered a "palmtop."
The device featured an integrated
mobile phone.

1995

RS02
Stackable tray set
Alessi
Italy

Mid-1990s

RICHARD AT THE F1 GRAND PRIX
Monaco

1996

KRYON
Computerized lighting
Artemide
Italy

THINKPAD 560
IBM
USA

The ThinkPad 560 had no floppy
disk, which made the device lighter
and more compact.

– IF Product Design Award, 1997

1997

COBAN
Coffee machine
Alessi
Italy

– Winner, Compasso d'Oro, 1998
– IF Product Design Award, 1999

1997

DESIGN CLASSICS: THE 9090
CAFETIÈRE BY RICHARD SAPPER
Edited by Sigfried Gronert
Verlag Form, Frankfurt am Main

1997

DESIGN CLASSICS: THE TIZIO-LIGHT
BY RICHARD SAPPER
Edited by Hans Höger
Verlag Form, Frankfurt am Main

1997

WEARABLE PERSONAL COMPUTER
Prototype
IBM
USA

– International Design Excellence
Award, 2001

[← P.86]

1997

THINKPAD 380
IBM
USA

– IF Product Design Award, 1998

1997

THINKPAD 770
IBM
USA

The ThinkPad 770 was a high-performance
model with a CD drive, substantial storage
and processing, and it was the first IBM
laptop to offer a DVD-ROM. As a result it
was so bulky that it was internally referred
to as the "phonebook."

– IF Product Design Award, 1998

1998

ORBITER
Office lighting system
Siteco Siemens
Germany

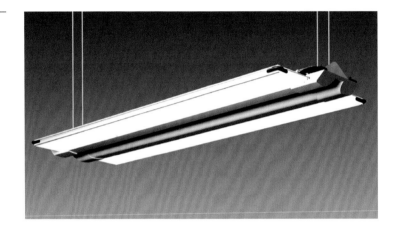

1998

INTERNATIONAL DESIGN YEARBOOK 13
Edited by Richard Sapper
Abbeville Press Inc., New York

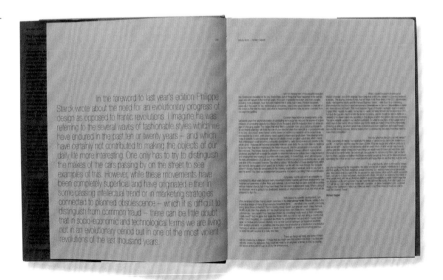

RICHARD WITH HIS STUDENTS
Stuttgart State Academy of Art
and Design, Germany

Richard is shown testing the project
Sapper-a-lot, by the design student,
Axel Schmid. The project was done
for a class taught by Ingo Maurer,
in which Maurer asked students
to build designs inspired by Richard's
Tizio Lamp. Richard was also a
professor at the Academy from
1986 until 1998.

[← P.81]

1998

THINKPAD 600
IBM
USA

The ThinkPad 600 was the first model
in the ThinkPad line to feature bevelled
edges, which made the laptop appear
thinner than it was. A single bay could host
an optical disk drive or floppy disk.

– International Design Excellence
Award, 1999

1998

HERE AND NOW AND LATER
Article by Michael Webb
Metropolis
February/March

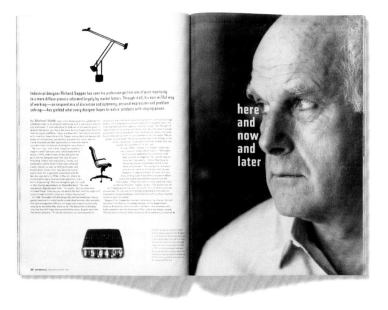

1998

THINKPAD I SERIES 1410
IBM
USA

This was the first ThinkPad marketed only
to individuals. An LED on the top of the
laptop's screen illuminated the keyboard
from above.

1999

LASER
Door handle
Olivari
Italy

THINKPAD 240
with Kazuhiko Yamazaki
IBM
USA

Late 1990s

RICHARD AND DORIT
Lake Como, Italy

1999

THINKPAD 570
Laptop computer
with Kazuhiko Yamazaki
IBM
USA

A detachable base, which held the
optical drive and additional ports,
could be removed to allow the laptop
to be more portable.

1999

AIDA
Stacking chair
Magis
Italy

[← P.87]

2000

NETVISTA X401
Desktop computer
with Kate Walker, David Hill, John
Swansey, Brian Leonard, Tony Latto,
and Bob Springer
IBM
USA

– International Design Excellence
Award, 2001

[← P.77]

2000

NETVISTA X41
Personal computer with pivoting arm
with David Hill, John Swansey, and
Brian Leonard
IBM
USA

– International Design Excellence
Award, 2002

2000

ZOOMBIKE
Folding bicycle
Elettromontaggi
Italy

– Winner, Compasso d'Oro, 1998
– IF Product Design Award, 2001

[← P.89]

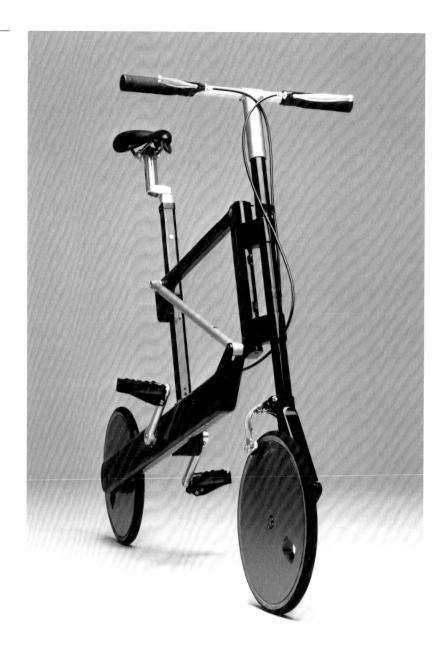

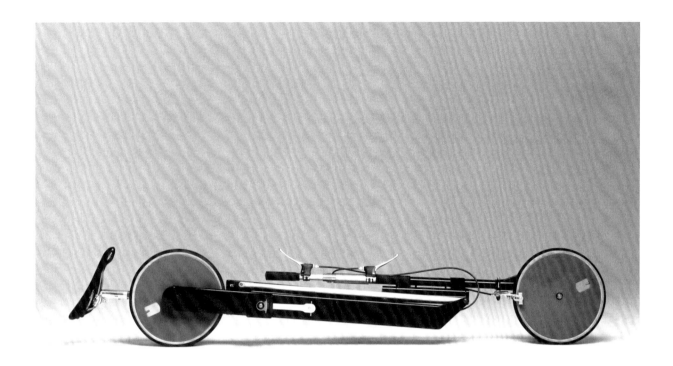

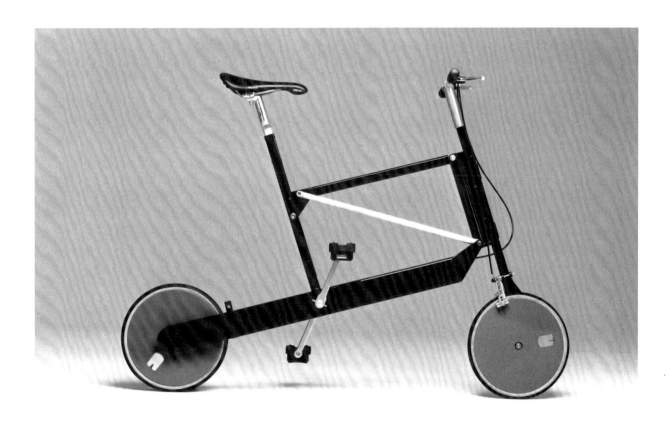

2001

AIDA FOLDING TABLE
Magis
Italy

[← P.87]

2001

THINKPAD A30
with David Hill and Tom Takahashi
IBM
USA

– International Design Excellence
Award, 2002

2002

RS07
Electrical espresso coffee maker
and Travel Set
Alessi
Italy

[← P.70]

2002

RICHARD SAPPER
by Michael Webb
Chronicle Books, San Francisco

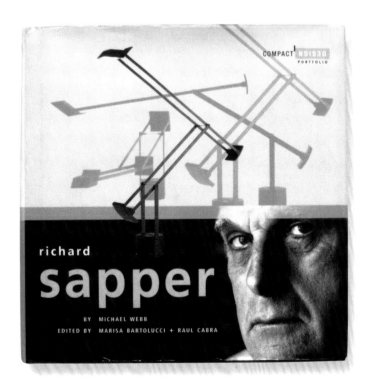

2002

T560
Flat panel computer display
with David Hill
IBM
USA

The T560 was an early flat panel
display, which replaced the cathode
ray tube (CRT) that was typical of
previous monitors.

– International Design Excellence
Award, 2002

2003

COAT HANGER
Prototype
Poltrona Frau
Italy

2003

DIALOG 1
Ballpoint pen
Lamy
Germany

2003

COVER INTERVIEW: RICHARD SAPPER
Article by Katsutoshi Ishibashi
Axis
Issue no. 103, May/June

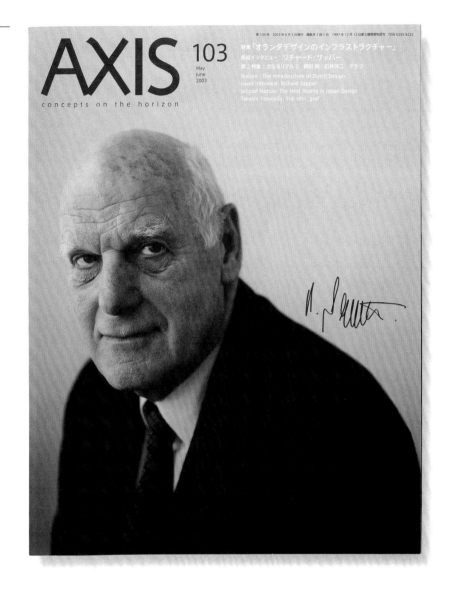

2003

ALA
Shelving system
Robots
Italy

2004

TODO
Cheese grater
Alessi
Italy

[← P.90]

2005

HALLEY
LED desk lamp
Lucesco
USA

[← P.90]

2005

DESK TOP COMET
Article by Peter Hall
Metropolis
April

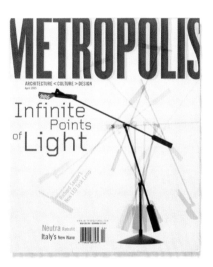

2005

RICHARD'S FIRST GRANDCHILD
LAPO IS BORN

2005

RICHARD SAPPER
Exhibition at Stilwerk
Berlin, Germany

2005

LENOVO ACQUIRES IBM'S PERSONAL
COMPUTING DIVISION

Richard continued his work as industrial
design consultant under the new ownership
of the personal computing division.
A design headquarters for this division
was established in Raleigh, North Carolina,
under the leadership of long time IBM
designer and close colleague of Richard,
David Hill.

2005

RICHARD RECEIVES THE "ARCHITEKTUR
& WOHNEN" DESIGNER OF THE YEAR
AWARD

2006

ARS09
Espresso coffee maker
Alessi
Italy

2007

RICHARD'S SECOND GRANDCHILD
CARLOTTA IS BORN

2007

RICHARD WORKING ON THE X300
From left to right: Richard, Tomoyuki
Takahashi, Kazuo Nakada, and Hiroki Hirano
Lenovo Design Center
Yamato, Japan

2007

RICHARD WITH HIS JAGUAR XK140
Lake Como, Italy

2007

THINKPAD RESERVE
Leather-covered laptop computer
Lenovo
China

2007

DESIGN INTERVIEWS: RICHARD SAPPER
by Francesca Appiani
in collaboration with Museo Alessi
Edizioni Corraini, Mantova

PER ME LA FORMA È LA CONSEGUENZA DI UNA VITA INTERIORE CHE DEVE AVERE L'OGGETTO

RICHARD SAPPER
Libro / DVD

2007

TOSCA
Stacking chair
Magis
Italy

[← P.87]

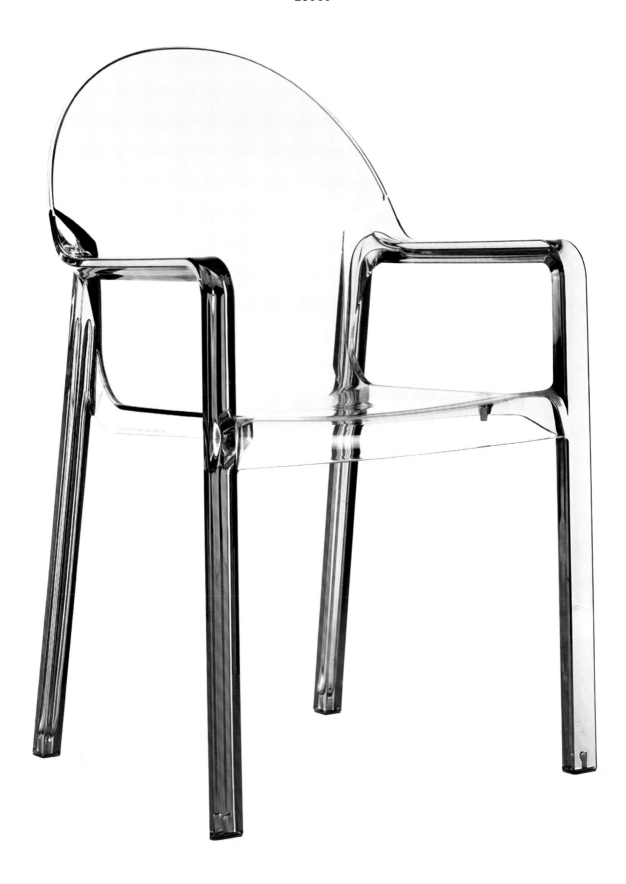

2008

LA CINTURA DI ORIONE
Kitchen knife set
with Alberto Gozzi
Alessi
Italy

2008

TIZIO LED
Desk lamp
Artemide
Italy

2009

SKYLIGHT
Smartbook computer prototype
Lenovo
China

RICHARD SAPPER

2009

RICHARD AND HIS GRANDSON LAPO
Lake Como, Italy

2009

RICHARD WORKING ON THE SAPPER
MONITOR ARM

From left to right: Dave Bloom, Ronald
Schneider, Richard, and Benjamin Pardo
Knoll Offices
New York, USA

2009

RICHARD RECEIVES THE "RAT FUR
FORMGEBUNG" LIFETIME ACHIEVEMENT
AWARD

2010

SAPPER MONITOR ARM COLLECTION
Monitor arm system
Knoll
USA

– Included in the permanent design
collection at the Museum of Modern
Art, New York

[← P.92]

RICHARD RECEIVES AN HONORARY
DOCTORATE
University of North Carolina, USA

2011

SAPPER MULTIPLE
Multiple monitor beams
Knoll
USA

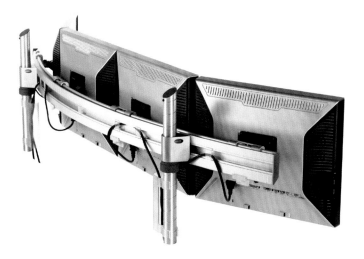

2011

RICHARD AND HIS GRANDCHILDREN
CARLOTTA AND LAPO
Lake Como, Italy

2012

RICHARD RECEIVES THE ORDER OF MERIT
OF THE FEDERAL REPUBLIC OF GERMANY

Presented to Richard by Joachim Gauck,
the President of the Federal Republic
of Germany

2012

THINKPAD X1 CARBON
with David Hill and Tom Takahashi
Lenovo
China

– IF Product Design Award, 2012

2012

TONGA
Electric salt and pepper mill
Alessi
Italy

[← P.79]

2012

RICHARD'S THIRD GRANDCHILD
TITO IS BORN

2012

SAPPER XYZ
Monitor arm system
Knoll
USA

[← P.92]

2013

RICHARD AND TOMOYUKI
TAKAHASHI OF LENOVO
Richard's home office
Milan, Italy

2014

RICHARD
Lake Como, Italy

2014

RICHARD RECEIVES THE ADI
(ASSOCIAZIONE DISEGNO INDUSTRIALE)
COMPASSO D'ORO LIFETIME
ACHIEVEMENT AWARD

2015

SAPPER SERVING TRAY
Design Memorabilia
USA

2015

RICHARD, DAVID HILL, AND TOMOYUKI
TAKAHASHI OF LENOVO
Richard's home office
Milan, Italy

2015

SAPPER DIES IN MILAN
December 31

2016

RICHARD SAPPER, 83, MAKER
OF CLASSIC PRODUCT DESIGNS
Obituary
Article by Sam Roberts
New York Times
January 10

Richard Sapper, 83, Maker Of Classic Product Designs

By SAM ROBERTS

Richard Sapper, an industrial designer whose sleek, precision-engineered prototypes spawned the Alessi espresso maker, the Tizio lamp and the IBM Think-Pad, died on Dec. 31 in Milan. He was 83.

The cause was complications of cancer, his daughter Carola said.

Mr. Sapper also designed for Mercedes, Fiat and Pirelli; conceived an ergonomic executive chair and computer monitor arms for Knoll; and invented tea-kettles that whistled in two keys, emulating an American locomotive. But he was especially revered by coffee connoisseurs for his lustrous stovetop Coban 9090 espresso maker, a graceful stainless-steel, single-piece machine that was introduced in 1979 by Alessi, the Italian housewares manufacturer.

The machine revolutionized home espresso-making, which had been dominated by the Bialetti model, an angular, narrow-waisted cast-aluminum design with a plastic handle. (The Bialetti was patented by an uncle of Alberto Alessi, now the company's president, in 1933.)

The Coban 9090 — named for the town of Cobán in central Guatemala, where Mr. Sapper's grandfather had harvested coffee — is now in the Museum of Modern Art's design collection.

By 2006, after 1.2 million Coban models had been sold, Alessi introduced an electric version modified to accept packaged pods of ground coffee beans, making it easier to use.

"For frustrated espresso drinkers, the new Alessi machine offers a nearly idiot-proof solution," Eric Asimov wrote in The New York Times.

Mr. Sapper influenced not only form but also function with another design, his linear Tizio desk-lamp, which helped introduce the halogen bulb in 1972. Later, his Halley model popularized the light-emitting diode, or LED (even though he personally preferred traditional incandescent bulbs).

That was not the only time he designed a product he preferred not to use. He also ground his own coffee beans the old-fashioned way, instead of using pre-measured pods. And in 1987 he collaborated with renowned chefs on a 23-piece, $4,000 Alessi cookware set, although, he explained, "All I can do is brew tea, boil an egg and grill steak."

Jonathan Olivares, a designer who wrote a book with Mr. Sapper, said Mr. Sapper's works were imbued "with warmth and poetry," each inspired by what he insisted was the requisite "kiss from the muse."

Richard Frank Sapper was born in Munich on May 30, 1932. His father, also named Richard, was an Impressionist painter. His mother was the former Carola Scherer.

In addition to his daughter Carola, he is survived by his wife, the former Dorit Polz; another daughter, Cornelia von Scheven; a son, Mathias; and three grandchildren.

After studying philosophy, anatomy and engineering, Mr. Sapper graduated with a degree in business from the University of Munich and began his career in the styling department of the automaker Daimler-Benz (now Daimler AG) in Stuttgart.

He later moved to Milan, where he worked for the architect Gio Ponti and in the design division of a department store. In Milan, he founded his own studio in 1959 and also began collaborating with Marco Zanuso on, among other designs, a cubelike portable radio for Brionvega and a molded plastic child's chair for Kartell.

Researching designs for a tea-kettle in the early 1980s, Mr. Sapper asked a cousin, who restored antique church organs, to come up with an instrument that could replicate the sound of an American locomotive he liked. The cousin produced a double-pitch pipe, and Mr. Sapper found a manufacturer in Bavaria to make it. The teakettle was called the Bollitore.

Mr. Sapper was credited (with Kaz Yamasaki) with IBM's first ThinkPad laptop in 1992 and (with Sam Lucente and John Karidis) with the svelte Think-Pad 701 in 1996 as well as (with David Hill and Tom Takahashi) the company's X1 Carbon laptop

His stovetop espresso machine transformed home coffee brewing.

in 2012. But he lamented that in Apple's infancy he had passed up an opportunity to do design work for the company's co-founder Steve Jobs because he was busy with other projects in Europe and did not want to move to California.

"Sure, I regret it," he told Dezeen, an architecture and design magazine, in 2013. "The man who then did it makes $30 million a year!"

Yet he bemoaned the influence of money on his profession, as industrial designers were becoming less likely to be hired by people who owned their own companies.

"Some of those company owners wanted to make good-looking things because there is pleasure associated with good forms," Mr. Sapper told Dezeen. "In many ways these people were idealists. They didn't make more money because they made a beautiful design. Today, it seems to me that money is the only reason to make design."

Mr. Sapper attributed a product's success mostly to "how it's marketed and presented to the public." But he offered some clues as to what constituted a classic.

"It's when the form of an object establishes contact with you, and you have to interact with it," he said. "I am very interested in objects that move and change character. That's the main theme of the Tizio, for example, or even the ThinkPad, which opens and reveals itself like a box of cigars. The Coban also has this nature — it makes noise, steam comes out of it, you see the condensation drops form. It starts to live."

Richard Sapper shown with his Tizio lamp and electric Coban espresso machine in 2000.

DESIGN Q&A

RICHARD SAPPER

For the exhibition *Qu'est ce que le design?* (What is Design?), which was held at the Musée des Arts Décoratifs, Palais de Louvre in 1972, Madame L. Amic asked Charles Eames a series of questions that would form the basis of the film that has since become known as the *Design Q&A*. These are the kinds of questions that should be reserved for designers who have reached maturity and worked throughout different periods of the human life span—in youth, middle age, and in seniority. After some fifty hours of conversation that Richard and I have logged in, it seems that anything we might have missed could be covered by these questions. And so, during our final lunch together, which took place at Musso & Frank's—a staple of old-world Hollywood that is past its glory days—I pose the questions to Richard, who has ordered the special: the bison rib-eye steak.

What is your definition of "Design"?
> It is the form of things mankind produces.

Is Design an expression of art?
> I would say yes, but it depends on the hands of the one who makes it. If it has passed through the hands of a great designer, it's art. If it has passed through the hands of the average corporate idiot, it's not.

Is Design a craft for industrial purposes?
> That is too limiting. I think that design is something very elementary. The best example I can give is the 10,000-year-old stone ax head that sits on my desk. It is a work of design made by a cave man. That object represents the answer to that question.

What are the boundaries of Design?
> I think a general answer on the boundaries of design cannot provide a solution that is always applicable. I can say, "I have here a project and these are the boundaries of that project." But then I might have another project, which has completely different boundaries. I mean, take the automobile for example: designing a Fiat Cinquecento has very different boundaries from designing a Rolls-Royce.

Is Design a discipline that concerns itself with only one part of the environment?
> No, design in its real essence is concerned with everything.

Is it a method of general expression?
> No. I think it's much more elementary. An understanding of design comes into focus at a museum with objects from the past 50,000 years of human development.

Is Design a creation of an individual?
> Could be, could not be. An individual can bestow an object with individuality, as opposed to it being anonymous.

Is Design a creation of a group?

>I think I have proved through my work that you do not need big teams to create innovation. As a matter of fact, big teams often act as brakes to innovation. However, you need big teams to translate innovative ideas into mass-produced products.

Is there a Design ethic?

>Yes. This is very complex. This is where Guardini comes into play.

Does Design imply the idea of products that are necessarily useful?

>Not at all. There have always been useless products, and there are now more than ever before. Then you have to define what the use of design is. If it is to make a beautiful object and that is the focus of this particular thing—he has created a beautiful object—then the use of that object is to be beautiful.

Is it able to cooperate in the creation of works reserved solely for pleasure?

>Sure.

Ought form to derive from the analysis of function?

>No. There are things that have no function and they are beautiful.

Can the computer substitute for the Designer?

>No.

Does Design imply industrial manufacture?

>It certainly does not.

Is Design used to modify an old object through new techniques?

>It can be.

Is Design used to fit up an existing model so that it is more attractive?

>No.

Is Design an element of industrial policy?

>It could be.

Does the creation of Design admit constraint?

>Yes.

What constraints?

>Well, constraints in the cost of the thing that you are making and all sorts of other constraints related to that. If you make a product of design, the creation of an object, you have to understand its limits...because nobody can make an unlimited thing. I think it's logical.

Does Design obey laws?

>Yes, the laws directing the proportions and the character of forms.

Are there tendencies and schools in Design?

>Yes.

Is Design ephemeral?

It should not be. Design should be something that is durable—the value of design should be durable. But naturally there can be situations where you make something and five years later you find out that it was stupid, so, you're not interested in that anymore. It was ephemeral. I'm interested in fashion, but only as long as it has lasting impact. It must stand the test of time.

Ought Design to tend toward the ephemeral or toward permanence?

I think permanence.

How would you define yourself with respect to a decorator? An interior architect? A stylist?

I am doing something different.

To whom does Design address itself: to the greatest number? To the specialists or the enlightened amateur? To a privileged social class?

It could be addressed to everyone, to posterity.

After having answered all these questions, do you feel you have been able to practice the profession of 'Design' under satisfactory conditions, or even optimum conditions?

Well, I would say satisfactory conditions.

Have you been forced to accept compromises?

Rarely.

What do you feel is the primary condition for the practice of Design and for its propagation?

Honesty.

"What is the future of Design?"

No Comment.

INDEX
BIBLIOGRAPHY

SELECTED BIBLIOGRAPHY

ARTICLES AND ESSAYS ON
RICHARD SAPPER

"Prefab—Una cella Bagno-cucina"
(Prefab—A Bathroom-kitchen
Module). *Domus*, February 1969,
p. 38.

George Finley, "People and Projects— IBM
Reorganizes Design."
I.D., May/June 1980, p. 16

Michele De Lucchi, interview with Richard
Sapper.
Ufficio Stile 14, 1982.

Deyan Sudjic, "Knoll's New Gang in Town:
Richard Sapper, A Cool Stylist," interview
with Richard Sapper.
Blueprint, May 1984, p. 20.

Patricia Leigh Brown, "The Tizio: Status
Icon of the 80s."
The Philadelphia Enquirer, March
17, 1985.

Lance Knobel, "Richard Sapper: Breaking
the Silence."
Designer's Journal, November 1985,
pp. 60–3

Paul Freiberger, "IBM's Road Machine."
PC World, August 1986.

Marco Romanelli, "Richard Sapper: PC
Convertible IBM."
Domus, July/August 1986
pp. 62–8.

Marco Romanelli, "Richard Sapper: Batteria
da Cucina, Officina Alessi"
(Richard Sapper: Alessi Cookware
Collection). Domus, October 1986,
pp. 58–65.

Chee Pearlman, "Where God Lives: An
Interview with Richard Sapper."
I.D., May/June 1991, pp. 32–7.

Piero Polati, "Intervista a Richard Sapper,"
interview with Richard Sapper.
*Il Modello nel design: La Bottega
di Giovanni Sacchi*. Milan, 1991.

Julie Trelstad, "Code Name: Leapfrog."
I.D., May/June 1993, pp. 70–3.

Michael Webb, "Here and Now and Then."
Metropolis, February/March
1998, pp. 58–63.

Katsutoshi Ishibashi, "Cover Interview:
Richard Sapper."
Axis, May/June 2003, pp. 56–61

Peter Hall, "Desk Top Comet."
Metropolis, April 2005, pp. 92–5,
138–9.

Steve Hamm, "Richard Sapper: Fifty Years
at the Drawing Board."
Bloomberg Business, January 9, 2008;
http://www.bloomberg.com/
bw/stories/2008-01-09/richard-
sapper-fifty-years-at-the-drawing-
board

Stephan Ott, "You Have to Rely on your
Instinct!" interview with Richard Sapper.
Goethe-Institut, June 2009;
http://www.goethe.de/KUE/des/prj/
des/dsn/stu/en4739094.htm.

BOOKS AND EXHIBITION CATALOGS
ON RICHARD SAPPER

Emilo Ambasz, *Italy: The New Domestic
Landscape*.
New York, 1972.

Uta Brandts, *Richard Sapper: Werkzeuge
für das Leben*
(Richard Sapper: Tools for Life).
Göttingen, 1993.

Gabriele Lueg, *Richard Sapper: Design*.
Köln, 1993.

Michael Webb, *Richard Sapper: Compact
Design Portfolio*.
San Francisco, 2002.

Francesca Appiani, *Design Interviews:
Richard Sapper*.
Mantova, 2007.

BOOKS ON INDIVIDUAL PRODUCTS

Alberto Alessi and Alberto Gozzi,
La Cucina Alessi
(The Alessi Kitchen).
Milan, 1987.

Sigfried Gronert, *The 9090 Cafetière
by Richard Sapper*.
Frankfurt am Main, 1997.

Hans Höger, *The Tizio-Light by
Richard Sapper*.
Frankfurt am Main, 1997.

Deborah A. Dell, *ThinkPad: A Different
Shade of Blue*.
Indianapolis, 2000.

Steve Hamm, *The Race for Perfect*.
New York, 2009.

BOOKS BY RICHARD SAPPER

Richard Sapper: 40 progetti di design
(Richard Sapper: 40 Design
Projects). Milan, 1988.

The International Design Yearbook.
London, 1998.

ARTICLES, ESSAYS, AND LECTURES
BY RICHARD SAPPER

"Modisch—Modern: Ein Problem der
Industriellen Formgebung"
(Fashionable—Modern: A Problem
of Industrial Design). *Graphik:
Werbung und Formgebung*, 1956.

"Design und Designer—Wozu Eigentlich?
Warum muß der Arbeitgebergeschmack
akzeptiert werden?"
(Design and Designer—Why
Actually? Why Does the Taste
of the Employer have to be
Considered?). *Bit—Büro und
Informationstechnik*, November
1982.

"Un futuro possibile"
(A Possible Future). Contribution
to a panel discussion with Ernesto
Gismondi, Vico Magistretti, Mario
Bellini, Richard Sapper, Gae
Aulenti, Cini Boeri, Ettore Sottsass,
and Michele De Lucchi during the
Salone del Mobile, 1983.

"Tizio"
Lecture during Westweek, Pacific
Design Center, Los Angeles, March
1987.

"The Design Process"
Pacific Design Center News,
May 1987.

"Filosofia e contenuto nel design"
(Philosophy and Substance
in Design). Lecture during the
conference "The meaning of design,
design management and patent
rights within the context of the
European market." EIMU
(Esposizione Internazionale Mobili
Ufficio), September 20, 1991

"Ist Design überhaupt lehrbar?"
(Can Design Even be Taught?).
Kontakte—Design Ausbildung,
catalog for the Stuttgart State
Academy of Art and Design.
Stuttgart, 1992.

"The Art of the Possible"
Design Review 2, 1993.

"Verkehrsformen—Die Mailänder
Verkehrsstudie"
(Forms of Traffic—The Milan
Transportation Study). *Werkzeuge
für das Leben*. Göttingen, 1993.

"Warum macht ein Designer Design?"
(Why Does a Designer Design?).
Werkzeuge für das Leben.
Göttingen, 1993.

AUTHOR'S ACKNOWLEDGMENTS

This book would not have been possible without the full cooperation and enthusiasm of Richard Sapper and his wife Dorit, who generously opened their lives to me, and imparted many invaluable lessons throughout the process.

I thank Ramak Fazel for providing the book's intimate visual introduction, and Marco Velardi at SM ASSOCIATI with his designers, Pietro Malacarne and Pietro Mazza, for providing the Italian flair that any good book on Sapper should have.

Richard's daughter Carola Sapper was most helpful in coordinating images, information, and translations of archival texts. Konstanze Essman, Danijel Losic, and Clara Marcenac, designers working in my office, were instrumental in compiling and editing the book's chronology. Maya Birke von Graevenitz at Phaidon produced numerous translations of archival Sapper writings and interviews.

David Hill and Tom Hardy provided information that helped me better understand Richard's working relationship with IBM and Lenovo, as well as the backstory behind the products he has designed for each company. Mason Currey lent his valuable eye as I was editing the Oral History. Justin McGuirk and I had some spirited dialog on Richard early in the book's process, and his 2013 interview with Richard for *Domus* magazine helped me convince the publisher that a book of this kind was needed. Thomas Demand gave me some vital editorial wisdom and his vote of confidence early on in the book's process.

For decades, Richard's friend and collaborator, the photographer Aldo Ballo, documented a large quantity of his work, and this book would not have been possible without the generous contribution of the Ballo+Ballo Studio. The book is further indebted to Marirosa Toscani Ballo for her support of Richard and Aldo Ballo's legacies.

My gratitude goes to Emilia Terragni, Joe Pickard, and Robyn Taylor at Phaidon for providing valuable input, support, and patience throughout the book's process.

Phaidon Press Limited
Regent's Wharf
All Saints Street
London N1 9PA

Phaidon Press Inc.
65 Bleecker Street
New York, NY 10012

www.phaidon.com

First published in 2016
© 2016 Phaidon Press limited

ISBN 978 0 7148 7120 2

Printed in China

A CIP catalog record for this book is available from the British Library.

Commissioning Editor:
Emilia Terragni

Project Editors:
Joe Pickard, Robyn Taylor

Editorial Assistant:
Maya Birke von Graevenitz

Production Controller:
Alenka Oblak

Translations:
Fiver Löcker

Design:
SM ASSOCIATI